THE ESSENTIAL ELVIS

THE ESSENTIAL ELVIS

The Life and Legacy of the King as Revealed Through Personal History and 112 of His Most Significant Songs

SAMUEL ROY & TOM ASPELL

RUTLEDGE HILL PRESS™
Nashville, Tennessee

A *Division of Thomas Nelson, Inc.*
www.ThomasNelson.com

Elvis Presley photos courtesy of Joseph A. Tunzi/J.A.T. Publishing

Published by Rutledge Hill Press, a division of Thomas Nelson, Inc.,
P.O. Box 141000, Nashville, Tennessee 37214.

Page design by Karen Phillips
Typesetting by E. T. Lowe, Nashville, Tennessee

Library of Congress Cataloging-in-Publication Data

Roy, Samuel.
The essential Elvis : the life and legacy of the King as revealed through personal history and 112 of his most significant songs / Samuel Roy and Tom Aspell.
p. cm.
Includes discography.
ISBN 1-55853-693-0 (pbk.)
1. Presley, Elvis. 1935–1997—Performances. I. Aspell, Tom, 1947– . I. Title.
ML420.P96R72 1998
782.42166'092—dc21 98–29204
CIP
MN

Printed in the United States of America
2 3 4 5 6 7 8 9—06 05 04 03 02

To my aunts, Sylvia and Rose, for their love and for keeping the poor boy well-nourished.

—Samuel Roy

Especially to my grandmother Margaret; my mother, Ethel; my father, John; and my wife, Barbara. And to Greil Marcus, the best rock writer of all time.

—Tom Aspell

The authors respectfully dedicate The Essential Elvis *to the memory of Robert Ammon, who died tragically from a sudden heart attack at age 42. This is our final chapter, Robert. Your energy, insight, love, humor, and friendship will always sing to us.*

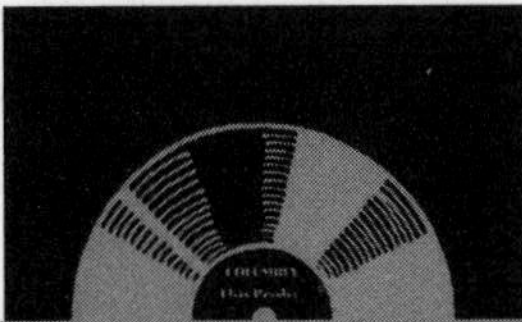

Contents

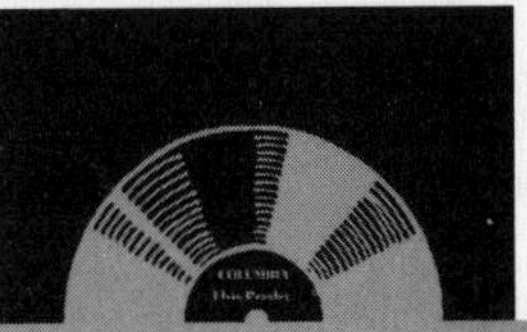

Foreword

By Gordon Stoker

I'm sure it doesn't come as a surprise to anyone that Elvis Presley mastered every style of music that he set his mind to. The young kid I first met at Memphis's Ellis Auditorium in 1955 (he had come to hear us perform with Eddy Arnold) really wasn't much different from the Elvis the rest of the world met on records, television, and in movies a couple of years later. He was always a professional, but at his best, he approached songs and projects with the enthusiasm of a 10-year-old.

I have so many strong memories of the Jordanaires' 15 years with Elvis. Many times, I saw him listen just once or twice to a demo record, and the next thing I knew, he was ready to record—and he'd nail the song on the very first take! I think he knew in his heart, even if he didn't really understand in his head, that perfection for the sake of perfection didn't count for much. He wanted a perfect *feel* on his records, more so than a perfect *take*.

Listen to my duet with him on "All Shook Up." We were singing on the same microphone, Elvis standing across from me, foot on a chair, slapping the back of his guitar to get that hollow beat you hear. The released take is pretty much perfect except for my final "yea yea," when I'm not quite in sync with him. I would've been, but he was goosing me and I lost my concentration at the end. When I said we should probably try it again, he laughed it off: "Man, if we haven't sold it by then, we're not going to. Forget about it." Of course, he was right.

The song reviews in Samuel Roy and Tom Aspell's *The Essential Elvis* are right on the money. If you're like me, the book will have you playing some of these records that you may not have heard in a while. I also have a new appreciation for the ones that I still hear a lot ("Teddy Bear," "Hound Dog," "Don't Be Cruel," etc.). But the interesting thing is that nothing much in this book would've made sense to Elvis. He *instinctively* knew what to do with his music, but I don't believe he wanted to think about it very much.

In many ways, this is the best book ever written about Elvis. Actually, it's the best book written about *what's important about Elvis*: his music. Why do we still love his music almost 50 years after he made his first records and more than 20 years after his death? Many have tried to figure out why, but Roy and Aspell have come as close as any of us are likely to get.

***Gordon Stoker** has been leader and first tenor of the Jordanaires since 1950. The group is known worldwide as one of the most versatile vocal quartets in music and has been together longer than any other vocal ensemble active today. The Jordanaires' sound has been an integral part of hit recordings by Patsy Cline, Ricky Nelson, George Jones, Johnny Cash, Roy Orbison, and countless other great stars, but they are honored to be best known for their legendary work with Elvis Presley.*

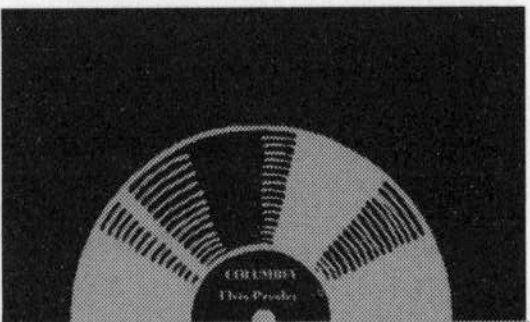

Acknowledgments

Thanks to Sam Roy's business partner and friend, Robert Ammon. Thanks also to the following, who contributed a great deal to this book: Barbara Lebeau, Edward Roy, Angela Roy, Robert Cole, Mona Joseph, Steve Carr, David Stobbe, Phil Gelormine, Andy Klein, Bobby Wysner, George S. Kasko, Steve Cvetan, President Bill Clinton for his inspirational comments on Elvis Presley, and Dr. Russell Scott for his advice. Sam Roy would also like to thank Karen Grenick, Dave Wolvin, Lynne McAllister, Rosanne Rendulac, Priscilla A. Parker, Lorraine Kursdorfer, Rowayda Michael, Juliet McDonald, Amy Leopold, Tom Esper, James Roy, Jimmy Roy, Michael Roy, Bill Roy, Richard Roy, John Rocco, Andrew Matsko, Ethel Matsko, Jeff Stanley, Ronald Supak, Dr. Robert Cohen, Richard Aiello, Krohmaly Printing, Homestead Business Machines, Rhamey Roy, Linda Hammond, Tom Milko, Dr. Louis Charles for the idea to become a writer, Dr. John Delaney for the inspiration to do this book, and Daniel Roy, a wonderful brother. Tom Aspell is grateful to his brothers and sisters: Kevin, Julie, Dennis, Anne, and Annabelle and Jack Barrett. And also to Caroline Barrett and Jeff Wyland and their son, Barrett, the "Little King."

We would like to thank many writers, but there is one who stands above the rest: Greil Marcus. Thanks also to our agent, Bob Silverstein, whose steady guidance and encouragement has been invaluable, and to John Mitchell, our editor at Rutledge Hill Press, whose incisive and respectful work made this a better book. Tom Aspell would also like to extend his thanks to the Insight Seminar and Support Group.

Special thanks to Joe Tunzi for the beautiful photographs he provided for this book.

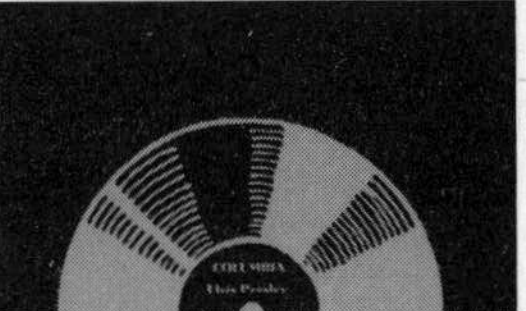

Introduction

The headliner on the marquee for the show of all shows is one man, one word: *ELVIS*! Elvis Presley remains the greatest musical and cultural force of the twentieth century. This critical and popular evaluation has been unjustifiably obscured since his death by the superficial tabloid and mainstream media, which have mythologized—often caricatured—him beyond recognition. Elvis's real legacy has been lost in the exploitation of those few sad, final years. Even the occasionally laudable coverage of the 20th anniversary of his death missed the crucial impact and musical prowess of the man and his music.

Our purpose for writing this book is to refocus attention on the power that Elvis's music, performances, and persona have retained—worldwide—for so long. Our special hope is that this work will introduce many young music fans to the man whose musical and personal magnetism broke down sexual, artistic, and even racial barriers, and enlightened our ways of relating to one another. Elvis shaped his resonant career from eclectic influences, as our essays document, yet hammered them, flaming, like a blacksmith, forging sound and fury into something new, something hard as steel and soft as secrets.

From the searing Sun sessions of the 1950s to the majesty and tragedy of 1977's live "Unchained Melody," Elvis spawned new cultural and musical traditions. The King's mystique is so embedded in the historical foundation of youthful rebellion that it is difficult to imagine what would be considered "hip" or "cool" today without him.

Elvis Presley was one of the pioneers of rock 'n' roll—wiring the wellsprings of blues, country, and gospel music to a huge transformer, then flipping a strange new switch and electrifying everyone from Tupelo to Tangiers, from Moscow to Mars. Yes, we do delve into Elvis's private strengths and weaknesses: sexual and romantic triumphs and failures, chemical dependencies, peaks and chasms of character. These revelations—many garnered from personal interviews conducted by Samuel Roy over the last 20 years—enlighten the link between Elvis and his music.

The songs and performances are often brilliant and profound; a great many are very good; and a few are uninspired or flawed.

This book is about the complexity of the man, the essence of spirit that has made Elvis Presley so captivating. It is also about his music and how that music reached—or didn't reach—us, and how it is inseparable from the man himself. The analyses are meant to be much more than just song reviews. They are portraits that reveal the real story about Elvis, his times and cultural influences, and how his career evolved. *The Essential Elvis* is also about America, about us, and about the world in which we live.

We have analyzed 112 songs for this book. Every essential performance is covered, as are those records we consider to be hidden gems. The other considerations are diversity and range. The songs are not reviewed chronologically or preferentially but are presented historically and artistically in ways that seem to best reveal the scope of Elvis's achievements and failures. We feel that trends and correlations are more important than just following a certain contrived order. Selecting a representative body of work freed us to follow our own direction.

Within the song analyses, we have designated album sources (vinyl and/or cassette) for collectors' information. Some of these recordings are currently out of print. The discography specifies where the songs are currently available on CD or cassette. Additionally, we have included obtainable chart positions for all of the singles and albums released during Elvis's lifetime.

We have carefully traced the waves of Elvis Presley's life and career.

THE ESSENTIAL
ELVIS

The Sun Years: House of the Rising Son

The man who would be King, Elvis Aron Presley, was born January 8, 1935, in Tupelo, Mississippi, to Vernon Elvis Presley and Gladys Love Presley. His twin, Jesse Garon, died at birth. The Presleys were as poor as church swallows. Vernon was a ne'er-do-well and somewhat of a pariah in the community. He stumbled through a variety of jobs, including a stint with the WPA, as if his work boots were two sizes too big. The Presleys, including Elvis, were lifelong worshippers of Franklin Delano Roosevelt, Jerry Schilling, a longtime friend of Elvis, confided to us. Without Roosevelt, the Presleys may never have survived the Great Depression. As a matter of fact, welfare paid for Elvis's birth. The charge was $15.

Vernon Presley once spent close to a year in jail for writing a bad $4 check. When Elvis made it big, no one was happier than Vernon, who could now live off of his rich and famous son. To the day Vernon died, he thought it was luck that had made his son so popular. When asked about this, Mr. Presley always drawled: "Weelll, it's kind of hard to say."

Some who had been close to Elvis recall that Vernon Presley was distant and cold—the antithesis of Elvis's mother, who was supportive, gentle and gregarious, full of life, a loving hospice. Elvis's devotion to his mother was so intense, it bordered on fixation. Their bond is legendary. She walked young Elvis to school into his teens. The first song that Elvis recorded at Sun Studios, "My Happiness," was a birthday present for Gladys.

Most researchers agree that Gladys made Elvis feel he was the center of the solar system, and this attitude was integral to his later success. Now, many sons and daughters are made to feel unique, but very few have ever been showered such motherly adoration as Elvis experienced. A philosopher once said that a trait relevant to all geniuses is that they feel they are men apart. Elvis always felt that way.

The Presleys were churchgoers, especially after 1937, when Gladys's uncle became the preacher at the local Assembly of God. It was in that church that Elvis witnessed the burning bush of gospel.

The sweeping, frenzied cadences and sweet, reverent testimonies charted his musical DNA.

Gladys Presley once made the comment that Elvis had the energy of three people. That Ulysses-like vibrancy is another insight into what made his records and concerts so invigorating. Another important point is that, as he grew up and in the early 1950s, Elvis truly felt like a free man. In describing some of his early hits, Dave Marsh, the famous critic formerly with *Rolling Stone* magazine and now working for *Playboy*, commented that "Elvis was the freest man in the history of fact or fiction." That sense of freedom was a key to Elvis's early music.

Elvis was very different from his classmates. He was a loner, an outcast who occupied the shadows of halls, rooms, and dances. People thought he was weird, a rebel, and these things set him apart. For instance, Elvis was kicked off the high school football team because he refused to cut his long hair.

The launching of Elvis Presley's musical armada has been documented so many times that we will cover only the essentials. Marion Keisker, an employee of Sun Studios in its heyday, liked Elvis's demo, "My Happiness." But Sam Phillips, the legendary studio's owner and producer, was not so enthusiastic. Phillips liked what he heard but was in no rush to call the youngster in for a session. However, every time Sam was looking for a singer to record a particular tune, Keisker would suggest Elvis. Finally, Phillips relented, and Elvis was summoned to the studio to cut two more records.

Elvis listened to all types of music—gospel, country, pop, blues—but so did others. What, then, inspired the transcendent magic he created during those supercharged sessions? It is our intent, in the pages that follow, to foster a better understanding of Elvis's accomplishments and their significance, both musically and socially, by examining the forces that motivated him personally and professionally throughout his career.

One thing should be understood: in the words of Dave Marsh, "Elvis was a public mute." Trying to solve the riddle of Elvis Presley by examining his interviews and comments in the media is a waste of time. His public modesty was a pretense, and most of his answers derived from what he thought people wanted him to say. Elvis participated in just two revealing interviews, and both of those, conducted by Hy Gardner and Wink Martindale, respectively, took place in the 1950s. In those interviews, he was cool, personable, and rebellious.

The inscrutability yet crystal clarity of Elvis Presley is indeed a Mystery Train that is still steaming through our days and nights.

♦ ♦ ♦ ♦

(**Note:** The songs analyzed in this chapter can be found on *The Complete Sun Sessions.*)

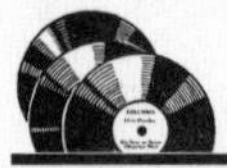

That's All Right (Mama)

Musically and socially, "That's All Right" is a landmark recording. It is on this song that Elvis first synthesizes black blues, white country and western, black and white gospel, and pop to produce a new and exciting sound. Elvis's voice sounds otherworldly, as if a sharecropper's plot has suddenly become a field of dreams where, if he sings, they will come. Scotty Moore's guitar percolates throughout, while Elvis's "Son, that gal you're foolin' with, she ain't no good for you" and the infectious "dee dee dee dee, I need your lovin' " drive the song home.

Elvis's elocution conveys a sense of freedom, both emotionally and technically. Anything could now happen, any time, any place. This song was the first crack in the dam, and it let the musical waters flow.

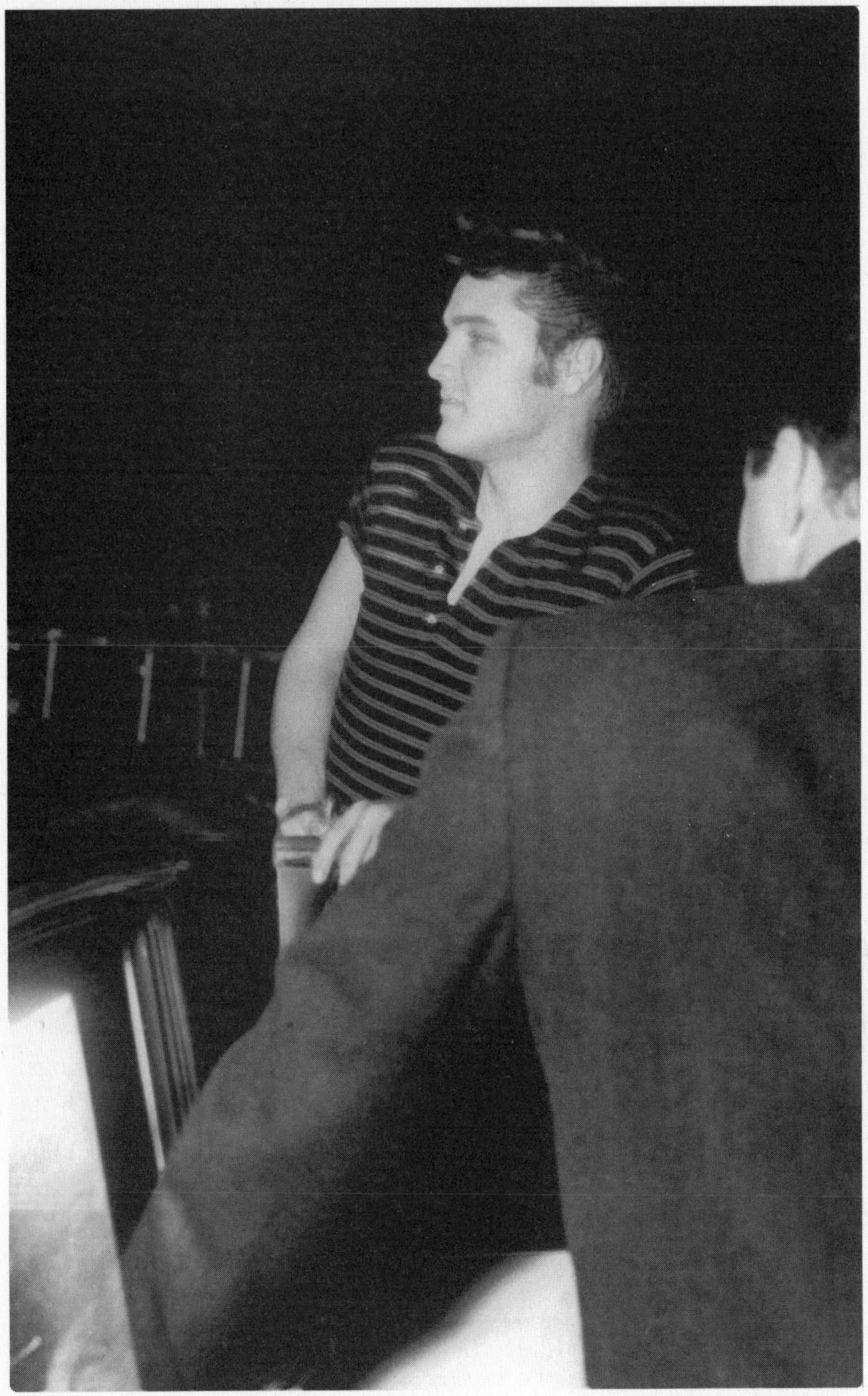

When "That's All Right" was first played on Memphis radio by Dewey Phillips, it was a smash. People kept calling and calling, requesting that it be played again and again. However, no one knew whether the singer was white or black, and there was an eerie silence about the issue.

Both Sam Phillips and Elvis knew that the mystery surrounding the song and its singer was enhancing listeners' interest. Close friend Eddie Fidal and others close to the fledgling star said Elvis was hurt by the charge that he merely copied from black artists, because he admired those musicians so much and knew it wasn't true. We feel this accusation unjustly diminishes Elvis's achievement of fusing black and white musical influences. Indeed, he helped pave the way for reciprocal changes in the dynamics of black and white relations, musically and culturally. He was largely responsible for a new perception of music as an instrument for creating large-scale social awareness.

Furthermore, Elvis was the first white man to top all music charts, including the black rhythm and blues lists. This gut-level reaction to the innovator and his music proves the amalgamation of spirits and styles was real and that Elvis was neither a fraud nor a mere imitator.

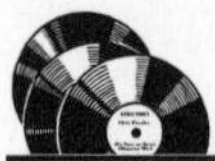

Good Rockin' Tonight

Elvis does much more here than prove "That's All Right" was no fluke; he makes the song rock 'n' roll. His straightforward singing, not just his intonations and inflections, creates an almost unbearable anticipation that is both influential and contagious. The "rock rock rock" vocal finale, repeated hypnotically and irresistibly, blows "all our blues away," breaking ground for a cultural superhighway that will cut through social restraints and inhibitions like a thousand bulldozers.

On this track, more than any other, Elvis puts his stamp on rock 'n' roll. The stretching of the art form's horizons is accomplished not only through his singing but also through the use of rock 'n' roll instruments and the manner in which they are played. Most important in this regard is how the lead guitar is used. The piercing, twanging sound perfectly augments Elvis as he belts out "Well, I heard the news—there's good rockin' tonight" with the visceral confidence of a visionary. Scotty Moore's pile-driving breaks elevate the guitar to a new and powerful position in rock music, while Bill Black's unique plucking bass parts imitate a whole rhythm section. There are no drums on this song.

It is impressive that anyone, let alone a boy of nineteen, could produce the drama found on this recording. "Hound Dog" and "Jailhouse Rock" are the sounds of a musical explosion, but connoisseurs should taste the pièce de résistance of "Good Rockin' Tonight."

The Russians would soon launch *Sputnik* (1957), but Elvis beat them to the punch, sending the entire world into orbit with a dynamic new sound.

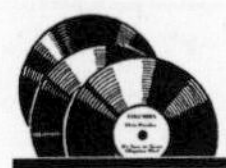

Blue Moon of Kentucky

Elvis nurtured this thoroughbred to run for the roses and played an essential part in the progression of country music. Bill Monroe, "the father of Bluegrass," who was recently enshrined in the Rock 'n' Roll Hall of Fame, wrote the song, which was released as the flip side of Elvis's first single, "That's All Right (Mama)." It represents an evolution in popular music, combining blues ("shine on, my woman has gone and left me blue"), country ("stars shinin' bright, wheat's growin' "), and the desperate urgency of gospel ("keep on shinin' "). The accents are on country vocal inflections and rhythm patterns, but there is a raw, uninhibited, galloping tension in the overall effect that challenges country forms while remaining true to them.

As is the case with all the recordings from the Sun sessions, there's a sense that something new is happening. The echo, undulations, and modulations in Elvis's voice are joyfully intense. Bob Dylan was inspired by this song, and its legacy can be heard in the work of artists ranging from the Beatles to Dolly Parton, from the Byrds to Gram Parsons. There has been a major country rock revival in the 1990s. Wynonna Judd, Garth Brooks, Billy Ray Cyrus, and Shania Twain can trace their musical roots back to "Blue Moon of Kentucky."

To this day, the sense of freedom in this song is inspirational. After Bob Dylan heard "Blue Moon of Kentucky," he knew that he would never work for anyone in his lifetime.

Baby, Let's Play House

Legendary rock guitarist Jimmy Page once said, "The record that made me want to play guitar was 'Baby, Let's Play House' by Elvis Presley . . . there was just so much vitality and energy coming out of it." Elvis's favorite instrument was the guitar, and he helped make it the most important instrument in rock 'n' roll. Here, Scotty Moore's muscular, jabbing guitar licks truly brought the instrument to the forefront of the combo sound.

Elvis's performance on this song did more to revolutionize popular singing styles than any other. Prior to Elvis, *all* singing was tightly controlled, in an emotional and technical context. That is not to say that earlier vocalists had not sung with passion. Billie Holiday, Robert Johnson, Judy Garland, Frank Sinatra, and many others delved deeply into the secret places of the soul, often cutting loose from the strictures of form.

But here, Elvis's inflections and mannerisms were so different,

so uninhibited and free, that he significantly challenged the conventions of all singers—black and white. Elvis's vocals gave other singers a plethora of new and exciting stylings to emulate and incorporate into their performances. Masterful but traditional "rule-book" singers had to change their styles because, compared to Elvis, they now seemed uninspired, even imprisoned.

Elvis invented the hiccuping effect ("come-a back-a, ba-by"), not Buddy Holly, Gene Vincent, or any of the other rockabilly imitators. Finally, the Pink Cadillac became a lasting symbol of rock 'n' roll!

The Sun singles were mainly regional (southern) hits, but Elvis's popularity continued to grow. No one had previously seen anything like his live performances, and audiences from the *Louisiana Hayride* to the shores of Lake Erie responded to the music and shows hypnotically, gasping as if they had seen a UFO. The tectonic plates beneath the earth's crust were shifting, and the tremors were affecting everyone's sense of balance. Snakes slithered into strange crevices; an alley cat was spotted burying a bone.

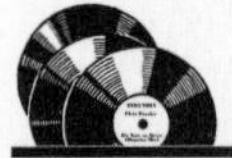

Milkcow Blues Boogie

If there is a particular moment when blues turned to rock, this may be it. Elvis starts out in slow, bluesy fashion—John Lee Hooker with a softer voice, maybe Mississippi Fred McDowell in a distant field—but then stops abruptly, slightly perturbed. "Hold it, fellas. That don't move me. Let's get real, real gone, for a change." This "ad-lib" was prepared in advance, according to rock scholars, but Elvis nonetheless delivers a seductive challenge, as if he senses the potential of these sessions and doesn't want to lose it.

On this record, Elvis achingly fuses the rigors of down-home country life ("ain't had no milk and butter since that cow's been gone") with romantic and class aspirations ("I'm gonna leeeave"). But as the lyrics conjure images of big-city lights, fame, and fortune, he still laments ("You're gonna neeeed your lovin' daddy here some day. . . . You're gonna be sorry for treatin' me this way").

Elvis cries out, "Let's milk it," just before Scotty Moore and Bill Black's instrumental heroics. Then, as if glancing back in hopes that his baby's comin' home—but discovering she's nowhere to be seen—Elvis turns the tables and takes his fate into his own hands ("Now I'm gonna tell you what I'm gonna do, I'm gonna quit my cryin', I'm gonna leave you alone, if you don't believe I'm leavin', you can count the days I'm gone"). It's not just the words that are convincing but the authority with which Elvis sings them.

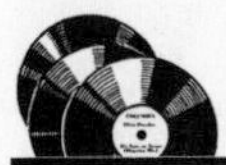

I'm Left, You're Right, She's Gone

This song is distinctive among the Sun recordings for two reasons. The first is that it relies heavily on drummer D. J. Fontana, thus completing the essential rock 'n' roll format of singer, lead guitarist, rhythm guitarist, bassist, and drummer. Only four songs on *The Complete Sun Sessions* use drums at all, and "I'm Left, You're Right" is the breakthrough. From Buddy Holly to the Beatles, the Rolling Stones and Byrds to Led Zeppelin and U2, this has been the basic rock-band lineup (Jimmy Page and U2's the Edge have utilized advanced technology and layering techniques to create multiple lead and rhythm texturing; the foremost master of this rhythm/lead dynamism was Jimi Hendrix). But it all started here.

Other instruments have been added, subtracted, or duplicated

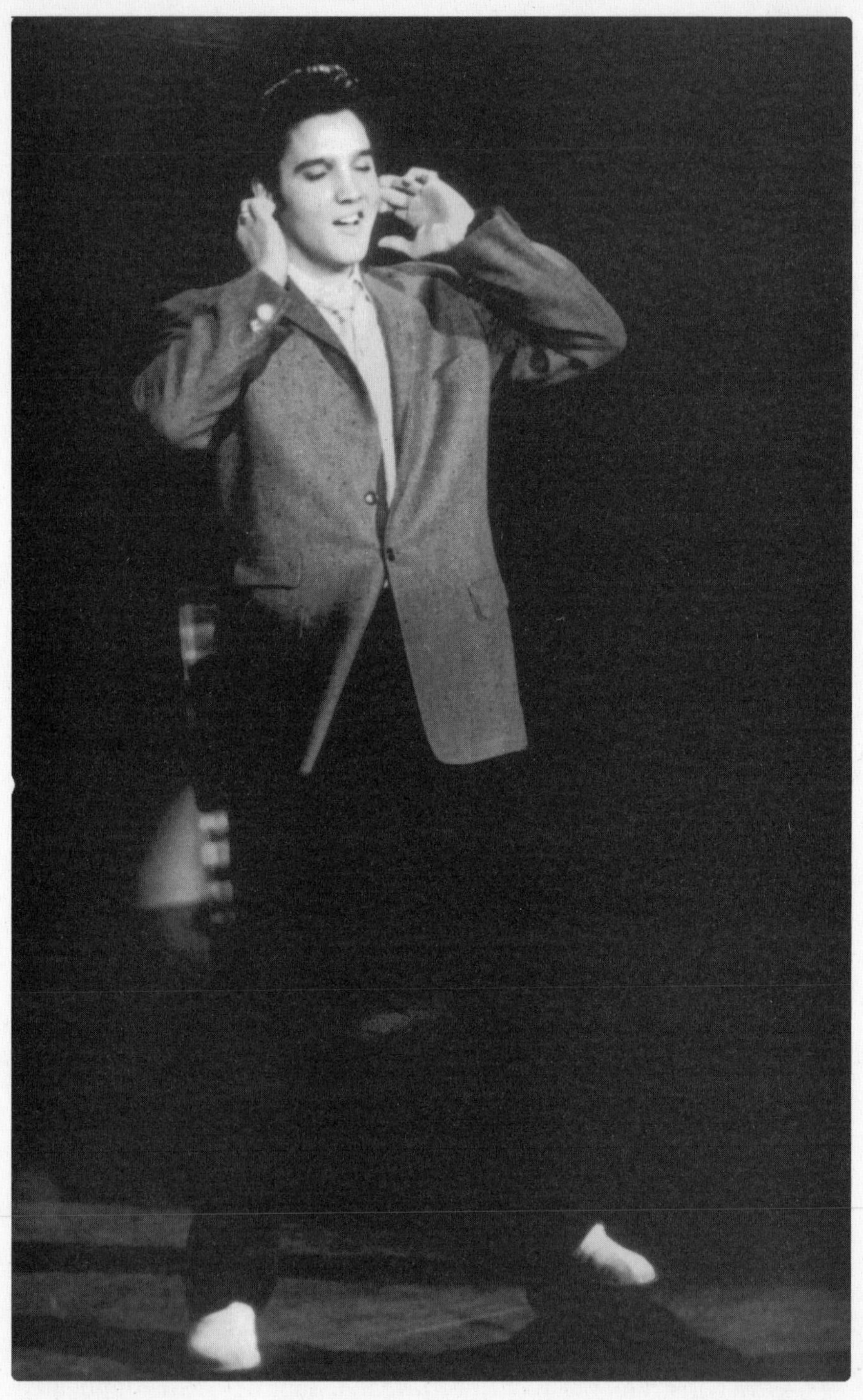

(through synthesizers and computer variations), but the ensemble featured on "I'm Left, You're Right" was the prototype. For instance, Bruce Springsteen at one time frequently utilized Clarence Clemons's saxophone as a lead instrument, but the nucleus of the E Street Band remained these founding rock 'n' roll instruments, with lead guitar in the role of dominance. Most renowned critics believe the Sun sessions as a whole represent the birth of rock 'n' roll. With Bill Black's magical bass and Elvis's rhythm guitar providing the backbeat, "I'm Left, You're Right" is really the cornerstone of the genre as we know it.

The second reason this song is so distinctive is that Elvis doesn't rely on a single blues influence but uses stylistic elements of the blues to shape rock 'n' roll. Many who charge that rock music is just another example of whites ripping off blacks simply don't want to give country and gospel their due credit in the development of this relatively new genre. "I'm Left, You're Right" isn't country music, but it derives some of its strength from the form. Similarly, "Tryin' to Get to You" owes as much allegiance to gospel music as it does to the blues.

Elvis's creativity during the Sun sessions may only be equaled by the Beatles' *Sergeant Pepper's Lonely Hearts Club Band.* His explosively free singing and forceful use of the rhythm guitar, along with Bill Black's wildly imaginative bass playing, liberated Scotty Moore's lead guitar to interject intense fill-ins, alternate runs, and chordal structures—making the lead guitar rock music's dominant instrument. For early blues monarchs such as Robert Johnson, Muddy Waters, et al, lead guitar was really the *only* instrument besides the voice. That's the difference between the blues influences and what the Sun sessions began to nurture. Critic Roy Carr calls the effect of this symbiosis "shattering."

Listen to the instrumental break on "I'm Left, You're Right"—one of the first full-fledged musical interludes of its kind in rock music. After Elvis sings "I've fallen for you," the guitar and drums kick in together, propelled by the bass, like an early experimental jet flirting with the sound barrier.

And Elvis is the coolest pilot in the sky as he then sings, devotedly, "I'll make it up somehow."

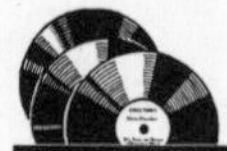

Mystery Train

This haunting performance of sustained tension and ease, seemingly set in the darkest part of the night, defines our deepest fears and doubts. Defiant, determined, and having fun, Elvis overcomes this challenge and takes hold of his own destiny.

The blues had always been about fatalistic hellfire music. Elvis broke through this foreboding of disaster and destruction. According to Greil Marcus in his book *Mystery Train*, the fact that Elvis took the guilt out of the blues but still made the music ring true was precisely his genius.

In his heyday, Pat Boone may have been an accomplished light ballad singer, but he didn't have a feel for rock 'n' roll or the blues. Hence, his singing reveals no guilt or passion; it isn't the blues or rock 'n' roll. Everyone has had the blues. Maybe we've even tried singing about it, but that doesn't make us blues singers. In order to sing any musical genre with authority, you have to understand the music and feel it in your bones. For instance, Wayne Newton sings all forms of music, but it all comes out as light pop. The distinguishing feature of the blues is unbridled confession; the focal point of rock 'n' roll is release.

"Mystery Train" is about a girl and her lover, and the fate of the mighty, dark, mysterious engine and sixteen coaches, which symbolizes all of our dread and secret dreams. In the blues world, this was something to fear—something that individuals had no control over. Before Elvis, the blues imprisoned men and women; they held no sway over their destinies and were victimized by things they could not change. One of Elvis's great gifts is that he took superstition and fatalism out of the blues. Blues singers would conclude that "the girl I love is on the train and it's gone," but Elvis seizes the train, the girl, and their destiny, then rejoices all the way home, declaring, "It took my baby—*but it never will again.*"

"Mystery Train's" roots lie deep within the blues tradition, but Elvis's fusion of blues and rock 'n' roll is carved like a lover's initials in this growing tree's sturdy trunk. The "train, train, comin' round the bend" is bound for fresh destinations.

Trying to Get to You

Compared with the blockbuster 1968 sit-down live edition, which is full of frustrated passion and eagerness, a mature lover dealing with quite complex emotions, this early studio recording shows a youthful Elvis in fine voice but a little too sure of himself to tap the potential of the song. It's performed in a bluesy rockabilly style with country strains—especially musically—but never blends these influences into a cohesive formula.

Elvis is obviously still experimenting with his sound and vision, which is fine, and there are some tasty moments, as when he sings "you really love me true," caressing the final word. Yet the technical command of his voice is too casual to match the required intensity of the words. Also, the band—especially the guitar on the break—is mixed too low, making the echo on Elvis's voice sound somewhat artificial.

Blue Moon

Extraterrestrial vocals backed by beautifully soft bongos and bass (the instruments are reminiscent of early *Gunsmoke* episodes) create an image of Elvis as lonesome cowboy, singing beneath a cold desert sky. The lyrics do not conclude with the joy of new romance, as in the Marcels' version. Instead, they drift toward oblivion, as Elvis's voice communicates calm acceptance despite the wrenching sorrow. A struggling, enigmatic, moving performance.

Elvis hits high notes like sparks exploding from a lonely campfire, hovering in the dark night air, then dissolving to dust. The blues scatting "wah, wah, wah . . ." before "without a love of my own" is similar to Janis Joplin's later wailing on "Ball and Chain" (1968), blending, burning into softness, resignation, rejuvenation. Janis once said, "Elvis is my man." Maybe they're sharing a couple of Southern Comforts at the Long Branch Saloon in a heavenly Dodge City.

♦ ♦ ♦ ♦

The fact that most of the songs from the Sun sessions had been recorded previously by black blues artists has led some to charge that Elvis Presley merely imitated black r&b performers. However, all you have to do is compare the differences between the bluesmen's versions and Elvis's reinterpretations to understand what a canard this assertion is. In most instances, they don't even sound like the same songs. As most respected critics in rock 'n' roll have said, Elvis did not steal his performances from black artists or anyone else.

Very importantly, as Dave Marsh and other musicologists have written, Elvis Presley developed a rhythmic pattern outside of r&b, a feat so challenging that it wasn't duplicated until the Sex Pistols did so in the late 1970s.

Elvis and Sam Phillips employed the band in ways that made the Sun sessions distinctive. For example, the visionary Phillips experimented with echo effects in the studio, which resulted in a haunting, ethereal quality in the music. That, and many more accomplishments, have made him one of the greatest producers of rock 'n' roll—perhaps second only to Phil Spector.

Vocally, and in the roles of bandleader and arranger, Elvis contributed heavily to the creation of his music. The stinging style he spawned on these recordings, we feel, is most influential. Sinatra swings soothingly, Dylan spits venomously, Bessie Smith eases our pain, Marvin Gaye gives us hope, but Elvis challenges us to overcome our limitations. His contributions are best articulated by Robert Hillburn of the *Los Angeles Times*: "Elvis mainly followed his instincts." One of the major reasons for Elvis's success is his ability to spark confidence. "Elvis was the biggest dreamer," Bruce Springsteen once mused, and those dreams, found throughout his music, are a secret formula. This is one of the reasons why, according to the first installment of *The Rolling Stone Record Guide*, "Elvis Presley is by far the most important single figure in the history of rock 'n' roll."

How good was Elvis's band in the 1950s? Despite some technical shortcomings, the group was good without Elvis but great when led by the King. For instance, there is positive proof that Scotty Moore is just not the same musician without Elvis Presley. Scotty did an album of Elvis's greatest hits, sans Elvis, but compared to the scorching, passionate sound he got when Elvis would tell him how he wanted the chords played, Moore's covers of the songs suddenly sounded tame and genteel. Elvis had the same effect on D. J. Fontana and, to a lesser extent, Bill Black, and other musicians and backup singers in the '50s. Black, via imaginative percussive bass overlays, contributed greatly to the Sun sessions.

Elvis learned a great deal about producing from Sam Phillips. What some critics don't realize is that by the time Presley signed with RCA, he was beginning to feel constrained by Phillips's blues-oriented productions. Elvis wanted a bigger sound to match the ambition and talent within him. And that's the key to the bold, undiluted sound he achieved during his recording sessions at RCA in the 1950s.

Despite the fact that Steve Sholes and Chet Atkins were listed as producers, in reality, their contributions were nominal. This is acknowledged in the rock world and documented by such authors as Alfred Wertheimer and Greil Marcus. Elvis ran his own sessions and produced them—something that was unheard of until he did it. Elvis accepted input from everyone, but his own mind conceived the distinctive sound that is a hallmark of those 1950s RCA records. He would listen to demo tapes, decide what he wanted to record, and then work out the arrangement, concentrating on the overall sound that he wished to create.

After cutting a song, Elvis would listen to it on a cheap record player. He said that his fans didn't have expensive audio equipment, and if the song sounded good on an old or low-quality turntable, then he knew it was done well.

This attention to detail was a key reason why Elvis Presley at his best (1950s, 1968–69) was the greatest singer and finest concert performer ever. In fact, a host of renowned critics and rock artists, from John Lennon, Bob Dylan, and Bruce Springsteen to Jim Morrison, Roy Orbison, and Pete Townsend, to name but a few, have commented that Elvis was the best of all time! Even through most of the 1960s and '70s, when he caught fire singing, Elvis was still the master, as evidenced by such releases as "Can't Help Falling in Love," "How Great Thou Art," "Hurt," and "Unchained Melody."

Considering all that he could do, it is barely worth a footnote to mention that Elvis didn't write his own songs. Some critics have contended that Elvis is somehow diminished as an artist because he didn't pen his own material. But such assertions are irrelevant, for the masterful way that Elvis changed the songs to create something completely new and different was far more important than writing them. Beyond that, some of the songs Elvis performed were so rewritten and sounded so different than the original versions or demos that they essentially became brand-new songs. For Elvis—like jazz greats John

Coltrane, Thelonius Monk, and Miles Davis—the *moment*, whether in the studio or in front of an audience, was like a burst of oxygen to a freshly struck match.

No significant songs were written by Frank Sinatra, Judy Garland, Billie Holiday, Enrico Caruso, Mario Lanza, Maria Callas, or Jerry Lee Lewis, yet their contributions to music are not doubted. Laurence Olivier and Jimmy Stewart didn't write their own scripts, and directors John Ford and Alfred Hitchcock didn't write their own screenplays, but their artistic vision has made their films memorable for generations.

Those who say that the music is not yours if you don't write it have no understanding of the production process or the ability of such artists as Elvis, Sinatra, and Jerry Lee Lewis to find so much more in a song than what the writer intended. As songwriter Doc Pomas once said, "Elvis always gets more out of my songs than I realized was there."

The Smithsonian Institution calls Elvis Presley "the most important voice in over 200 years of American music." Truly great songwriters, Bob Dylan among them, have made tremendous contributions to American and/or rock music, but none, with the exception of John Lennon and Paul McCartney, have left their mark on the art forms as deeply as did Elvis Presley and Louis Armstrong. Elvis did it with his voice, sound, and production; the Beatles did it with their songwriting and studio pyrotechnics; and "Satchmo" altered the shape of popular music instrumentally.

To further dissolve the pointless argument that Elvis should be devalued as an artist because he didn't write his own songs, Greil Marcus writes that "Elvis Presley was talented in a way that no one else in this century was talented."

CHAPTER 2

The Fabulous Fifties: Breaking the Sound Barrier

By the mid-1950s, it was clear to many in the industry that, like the hottest new car in American history, the Ford Thunderbird, Elvis Aron Presley was on the road to becoming a national phenomenon, or a new Frank Sinatra. The one person who did not understand this was Sam Phillips—for in one of the great blunders in the annals of music, Phillips sold the rights to Elvis to RCA Records for $35,000, plus a $5,000 signing bonus for the rising star. That would be akin to optioning a young Michael Jordan, after his first year in the NBA, for $200,000. Amazingly, Phillips thought he had a singer under contract that he could make into another Elvis Presley. The kid's name was Carl Perkins, and the idea was preposterous.

As *Rolling Stone* critic and *Elvis* author Jerry Hopkins documented, the King didn't just take the money and run to the big time. As Phillips himself verified, Elvis told the venerable producer that he would gladly stay with Sun if that would be in Phillips's best interest. The truth is, while $35,000 seems like a paltry sum today, it was a veritable fortune in 1956—and Sam needed the money. Of course, he ultimately lost out on countless millions of dollars.

Elvis did not enter the RCA studios with the intent of copying the Sun sound, except where the echo effects were concerned. No, the kid from Tupelo had some bold ideas for his new records.

However, according to historians' "great man" theory, ideas frequently are not enough; to achieve greatness, one must be favored by both the times and opportunity. For instance, would Lincoln have been great without the Civil War? Would Roosevelt have been so impressive without the backdrop of the Great Depression or the Second World War? Elvis also benefited from both the times and opportunity.

The youth of the 1950s had no real music, language, style, or form of expression they could call their own. As all previous generations had done, they listened to the music of their parents: Frank Sinatra, Perry Como, Vic Damone, Patti Page, Nat "King" Cole, Louie Prima, and Keely Smith. However, the times were changing.

The depression and World War II had been over for some time, and the economy was strong; people had money to spend on new homes, automobiles, and the latest appliances. The economy was so bullish, the United States was actually exporting oil. Schools were being consolidated, and many a teenager owned his own jalopy. Youngsters actually had money to spend and were itching for something new into which to channel their restlessness. There was peer pressure; what had been handed down was no longer good enough.

The white youth of the mid-1950s were looking for something more exciting than the American Dream they already possessed. Some found it in rhythm and blues music, but r&b was not played on major radio stations, and it wasn't explosive enough.

Things changed dramatically in 1954, however, when a journeyman country singer named Bill Haley decided to give this primitive rock 'n' roll music a try. When he released "Rock Around the Clock" that year, the world listened. There were many big-band elements in the song, but American teenagers found the new sound to be infectious. Haley was white; thus, he was more accessible to white audiences than were most r&b artists, but he was neither charismatic nor a great talent—so, although he was a forerunner of a new musical style, Haley quickly faded from the scene.

On the silver screen, Marlon Brando and James Dean captured the spirit of youthful rebellion better than most of their peers. Elvis was a big fan of both actors—especially Dean—whom he called a "genius." But even when *Rebel Without a Cause* was released, parents, particularly mothers, took their children to see the movie. While Dean was indeed the "first teenager," he did not spawn "youth culture." Very soon, Elvis would set the standard by which everything cool was measured—he would become what most teenagers aspired to be.

The fact that Elvis Presley became as popular around the world as he was in America, even in places that weren't so prosperous, proves the legitimacy of his work. People in countries where virtually no English was spoken felt his magic and responded. As Bruce Springsteen once observed, "Everything starts and ends with [Elvis]. He wrote the book."

In 1956, gas cost 22 cents a gallon, Glenn Miller and Tommy Dorsey were household names, and a young United States Senator named John Fitzgerald Kennedy lost the Democratic vice-presidential nomination to Estes Kefauver, the renowned Senate crime fighter. A dramatic but successful bus boycott was implemented by blacks in Montgomery, Alabama, and a 26-year-old reverend named Martin Luther King Jr. became the leader of the Civil Rights movement. Although Joseph McCarthy had been censured by the Senate, the blacklisting of suspected Communist sympathizers continued in many places across the country. Americans loved watching Lucy on their black-and-white television sets, but they lost their infatuation with Uncle Miltie. Elizabeth Taylor was involved in her second marriage, while Mickey

Rooney was going through his fourth. An elegant and beautiful American, Grace Kelly, was officially invested as Princess of Monaco, and John Travolta celebrated his second birthday.

The year 1956 was also the year that an earthquake named Elvis Presley would forever change America and the world.

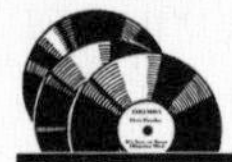

Heartbreak Hotel (*Elvis: Worldwide 50 Gold Award Hits, Vol. 1*, 1970)

Elvis's first RCA single, released in January 1956, included all the innovations of the Sun sessions but presented something entirely new: a sound so big and so different that people around the world sat up and took notice. With "Heartbreak Hotel," Elvis essentially announced that nothing would ever be quite the same again. Imagine the impact this song made as it blared from the speakers of a Chevy Bel Air at a drive-in burger palace or wafted from the family Philco as high school sweethearts snuggled nervously on a porch swing at night.

Elvis's vocal is big, sullen, sensual, brooding, and bluesy. There's an eeriness, a desolation that stings the spine like whiplash after a crash in the middle of nowhere. His cry of pain ("Well, since my baby left me") literally shakes radios and Victrolas across America, then shrinks to almost nothing ("I'm so lonely I could die"). There has rarely been a more riveting portrait of lost love than "Heartbreak Hotel." It also represents the dawn of rock 'n' roll to the popular consciousness. Scotty Moore's guitar break after "you'll be so lonely you could die" cuts like a scalpel, while Bill Black's bass is a fading heartbeat and Floyd Cramer's impeccable piano sheds tears of loss.

This song influenced countless future musicians, and elements of its haunting grace can be found in many songs and recordings produced since. One example out of hundreds is "Hotel California" by

ELVIS PRESLEY

the Eagles ("You can check out anytime you please, but you can never leave"), which was released about 20 years after "Heartbreak Hotel." The sensuality evoked on the original marked the rise of Elvis Presley as a major sex symbol.

"Heartbreak Hotel" can still be heard on local radio stations as you drive through Baton Rouge, Memphis, Los Angeles, St. Louis, and many other cities. When it comes on, adjust all your mirrors.

I Was the One *(Elvis: Worldwide 50 Gold Award Hits, Vol. 1,* 1970)

Top-notch lyrics, at once clever and soulful, are rendered with delicate panache by Elvis, who is supported well by the Jordanaires' backup vocals and a somber yet earthy piano, drums (featured instruments), bass, and guitar. The opening guitar notes are high and jarring, almost like a piercing alarm clock awakening Elvis from a restless dream that he must relate to the listener. The "do do do do" chorus kicks in before Elvis intones "I was the one who taught her to cry," perfectly timed, low and soft, while an insistent piano pings like partially frozen rain on a roof. The drums are muffled and the guitar is toned way down throughout the rest of the song, taking center stage again only after Elvis's final aching "I was the one," and then serving as a gentle counterpoint to the singer's regret.

This stellar 1956 cut is often overshadowed by many other monster RCA releases from that golden period. It shouldn't be—it can hold its own against most of them. The line "she lived, she loved, she laughed, she cried" would have been over-dramatized by many other singers, but Elvis keeps it steady, turning the sentiments inward, almost as if singing about himself, yet still focuses on her—and that's the strength of his interpretation. There is no self-pity here, only glimpses of anguish as his voice stutters slightly on "I . . . I'll never know who taught her to lie."

Later, as the Jordanaires croon "wah wah wah coo" like uptempo Perry Comos, Elvis sings "and theeen one day, I haaad my lover," elongating the vowels in "then" and "had" as if trying to tune in a song from a distant AM station. It's an inspired technique—one with a purpose. Who "learned a lesson when she broke my heart?" Elvis is the one. And so are we.

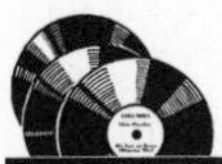

Hound Dog *(Elvis: Worldwide 50 Gold Award Hits, Vol. 1, 1970)*

This is one of the most important songs Elvis recorded during the 1950s—and one of the most controversial.

A number of critics, from columnist Carl Rowan to novelist Alice Walker, have used this song to disparage Elvis's authenticity. Walker wrote a short story based on the alleged circumstances surrounding "Hound Dog." Not only was her basic thesis misguided, several of her assertions were incorrect. For instance, she was off the mark in claiming that the black woman who first recorded the song, Willie Mae "Big Mama" Thornton, also wrote "Hound Dog." Certainly, Walker should be commended for defending black artists who have been exploited by the music power structure; however, we believe Elvis's rendition of "Hound Dog" is not exploitation but extension, a reformation of what came before.

According to Greil Marcus and others, the song was written by Jerry Leiber and Mike Stoller, both white. They looked to a white blues singer, Jim Otis, to record the tune, but Otis passed it on to Thornton. Otis attempted to take writing credit for the song, and Leiber and Stoller had to fight a legal battle to win back complete composing credit.

The version that Leiber and Stoller wrote—and which Thornton recorded—was not the same song, lyrically or musically, that Elvis released. The only line in the original version of "Hound Dog" that Elvis used on his record was "You ain't nothin' but a hound dog." The music was changed just as dramatically and bears no resemblance to the Thornton version.

Here's the true story: Several reliable sources, including Dave Marsh, relate that a Tin Pin Alley band performed "Hound Dog" in a lounge, speeding up the tempo dramatically and playing the song as a complete joke. Elvis thought the song needed a faster tempo, but not the kind he had heard in the bar. The King retained the pacing—and meaning—of the original but changed the words and tempo, turning "Hound Dog" into a menacing protest against lame conformity.

A great artist takes what is there and makes something new out of it. Elvis saw "Hound Dog" as the perfect vehicle to express his vision, rebellion, and ambition. When Steve Allen tried to make a national joke out of Elvis by forcing him to sing—wearing a tuxedo—to a real hound dog, it infuriated the young performer. The very next day Elvis recorded "Hound Dog," and that anger, visible in Elvis's face while he had performed "Hound Dog" on *The Steve Allen Show*, became a jackhammer in his voice and heart.

The sound and performance Elvis created for "Hound Dog" have been likened to an "earthquake," a "cataclysm for which no one was prepared" by Greil Marcus, and a "prison riot" by Jim Miller in *Newsweek*.

Elvis's performance of "Hound Dog" was a drastic break from the status quo, both in terms of musical expression and the social reaction it engendered. Elvis and his band form an army of sound: Bill Black's bass reinforces the song's forceful stance and provides its driving rhythm, pumping energy into Elvis and the music. Scotty Moore's guitar adds a gutsy, riotous sound that harasses and offends some listeners while simultaneously enticing others.

The players mimic Elvis's disdainful approach. At the end of each verse of the song, everyone else steps aside while Elvis punctuates

words like a boxer punching a speed bag. Then, D. J. Fontana barrages the listeners with supercharged triplet patterns, hammering the message home, then stops dead with a hard bass-drum kick, ending that message and foreshadowing a new one. The instant after Bill Black's bass challenge, Elvis cuts in with another verse, driving the song to its close.

Moore's hard-strumming guitar break on "Jailhouse Rock" after Elvis cries out "rock rock rock rock" sounds like a bitch in heat and is often credited with setting the standard for rock 'n' roll guitar playing. His punctuated strumming and stinging notes on "Hound Dog" almost match that intensity as the growling and biting notes spur on Elvis's ferociousness. This interplay gives the song its structure and vivid presence.

The Jordanaires' clapping adds to the hard-driving sound, giving it a certain fullness, yet it seems to throw everything off balance—they're almost out of time. They sing harmony behind Scotty Moore's guitar solo, keeping the full sound intact but adding a little sweetener, so the song doesn't lose its appeal. Their "ah ah ahs," at once blissful and painful, provide a contrast to the guitar, which gives the rhythmic licks and the singing patterns greater emphasis. The pronounced expressions heard in this song are absorbed from a number of musical sources that effortlessly come together to form a unique and tightly knit production. It is one blast after another.

But it is Elvis's voice, as explosive as a land mine in suburban America, that gives the song its special quality. The King strikes back at every critic and self-appointed arbiter of good taste who ever had attempted to dethrone him. He is so determined, undaunted, and confident that he gives the impression that anything can be overcome.

It should be noted that, while Elvis completely rewrote the lyrics and music to "Hound Dog," he accepted no writer's credit. Elvis, Jerry Leiber, and Mike Stoller ultimately made a small fortune on the song, and they formed a relationship that led to many successful records. But Leiber and Stoller never gave their best material to Elvis, e.g., "Stand By Me" (they didn't write it, but they chose the artist to record it), "Kansas City," and others. Big Mama Thornton's "Hound Dog" is fine r&b, but Elvis's "Hound Dog" is a work of rock 'n' roll alchemy.

♦ ♦ ♦ ♦

Just as John F. Kennedy was the first "media president," Elvis Presley was the first entertainer who knew how to use television. His appearances on the most popular TV showcases of the day—*The Dorsey Brothers Stage Show, The Ed Sullivan Show*, and *The Milton Berle Show*—forever altered the status quo in society. Take Elvis's first nationally televised appearance on the Dorsey show: To many, he appeared to be a creature from another galaxy, yet he was still the boy next door. His four-piece band was louder than the entire Dorsey orchestra, and his gyrations were so appallingly sexual that no one was prepared for them. The energy coming from Elvis and his music reduced the feeling of distance created by TV and brought the charismatic star into homes all across America.

His three performances on *The Ed Sullivan Show* moved the censorship issue—previously concerned with sleazy movie houses and magazines, and Supreme Court rulings—from the editorial pages right into our living rooms. Amazingly, during Elvis's first two appearances on the show, his entire body was shown on camera while he performed. The quintessential array of middle-class Americans gathered around their televisions on those Sunday nights at 8 P. M. Eastern was transfixed yet horrified at the same time.

But as shocking as Elvis's moves were on the Dorsey and Sullivan shows, his performance of "Hound Dog" on *Milton Berle* set off fire alarms. His gyrations were so outrageous and daring that they marked the widest break from shared culture that Elvis would ever achieve.

The censors struck during his third Sullivan appearance, and Elvis was out—the cameras showed him only above the waist. But, somehow, Elvis made this the sexiest of his Sullivan incarnations—"You can't see, can't feel me now, baby, but wait till we get to my place," was the invitation he seemed to extend with every word, every gesture.

Elvis's early television appearances on Dorsey, Sullivan, and particularly the Berle show were defining moments of seduction and allure in American popular culture.

Don't Be Cruel (*Elvis: Worldwide 50 Gold Award Hits, Vol. 1*, 1970)

What a sound! It is so precise, so light, so balanced that only a dozen recordings in rock history have captured anything close to its essence. The way Elvis meshes his voice with the music and the Jordanaires is magical. His nonchalance and confidence are playfully seductive.

Greil Marcus, arguably rock 'n' roll's most brilliant writer and critic, wrote in *Mystery Train* that the genius of Elvis's singing is his capacity to combine ease of delivery with an intensity that has no parallel in American music. This is the King at his best—whether he's singing "Hound Dog," "Don't Be Cruel," "Hurt," or a wealth of other songs. Elvis could infuse lyrics with great passion, but he could also create an island of peace, a sense of relaxation in the center of the storm. That is why his songs don't wear thin on repeated listenings.

The flip side of "Hound Dog" when it was released in 1956, "Don't Be Cruel" became a huge hit in its own right. It showcases Elvis in one of his coolest moments, rivaling "You're So Square" and "Baby, Let's Play House" as an evocation of the hip attitude that many young males of the '50s and beyond dreamed of having—while many young women fantasized. He is disarming, displaying vulnerability ("If you can't come around, at least please telephone") and playfulness. The "mmmm" after ". . . you I'm thinkin' of" is gorgeous in its casual anticipation of reunion, before the song shifts to the confident urgency of "Don't make me feel this way."

The ending is sweet yet forceful, varying in temperature like the layers of a hot fudge sundae. "Don't Be Cruel," repeated, is followed by the Jordanaires' "oooooos," then Elvis bursts out strongly, "I don't want no other love!" His delivery is full of heat, as if to show his woman that the earlier "Let's walk up to the preacher, and let us say I do" (punctuated by the Jordanaires' "bop bop bop") was sincere. The last line, "Baby, it's still you . . . ," is soft and breezy as a soda shop with its doors wide open on a sticky summer night.

Suddenly the jukebox plays A-16. Those tight bass notes kick in, and everybody gets up to dance. Everybody except for the guy wearing sunglasses and a black T-shirt, and the strawberry blonde with the pink pumps, who sit quietly, gazing into each other's eyes.

♦ ♦ ♦ ♦

"Don't Be Cruel" brings up another black and white dispute. Otis Blackwell wrote the song and is angry because Elvis became so successful but never took the black performer on tour. Of course, he doesn't mention that the Sweet Inspirations, a black soul group, opened for Elvis for many years. Blackwell is jealous because he feels that he made Elvis, even going so far as to claim that Elvis just copied his demos and went on to fame and fortune, while Blackwell was ignored and ripped off because he was black (although he did make royalties).

Blackwell took his case to talk-show host David Letterman—who was only too happy to see Elvis put down. After telling everyone that the King copied his demo of "Don't Be Cruel," Blackwell said he could prove his case and proceeded to sing the song. Anyone not intimately familiar with the words would not have recognized the song. There was no freedom or ease, and certainly no magic. Spitting the words out, Otis sounded as if he were angry at the song. It sounded nothing like Elvis's version.

There is another myth that needs to be debunked. Some have charged that Elvis copied his on-stage movements from Bo Diddley after seeing the entertainer perform at New York's Apollo Theater in 1956. That can't be true, since Elvis was performing his distinctive movements on stage for two years prior to seeing Diddley. Moreover, as Diddley's performance on *The Ed Sullivan Show* documents, his moves were tame compared to the King's.

It is a fact that many black artists have not received proper critical or financial rewards for their artistry. During the 1950s and '60s, royalties were sometimes withheld from black songwriters and performers, and artistic appreciation often amounted to categorization at best. James Brown, for example, is known as the "Godfather of Soul," but he is rarely referred to or acknowledged as simply a great singer/performer. Therefore, the bitterness directed toward Elvis Presley, as a successful white performer, by certain members of the black community is understandable. However, charges that Elvis imitated black performers vocally and musically, copied their mannerisms, or denied them credit for their work are simply unfounded.

When Arthur "Big Boy" Crudup, the writer of "That's All Right (Mama)," needed backing for studio time in the late 1960s, Elvis gave him $4,000. This was not done out of guilt; rather, it was an expression of deep caring and appreciation for someone who had helped inspire Elvis to express himself in his own ways.

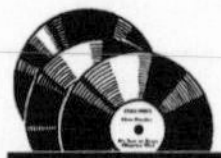

Tutti Frutti (*Elvis Presley,* 1956)

This recording pales next to Little Richard's original, which is turbocharged with wild, almost hysterical sexual frenzy, and created

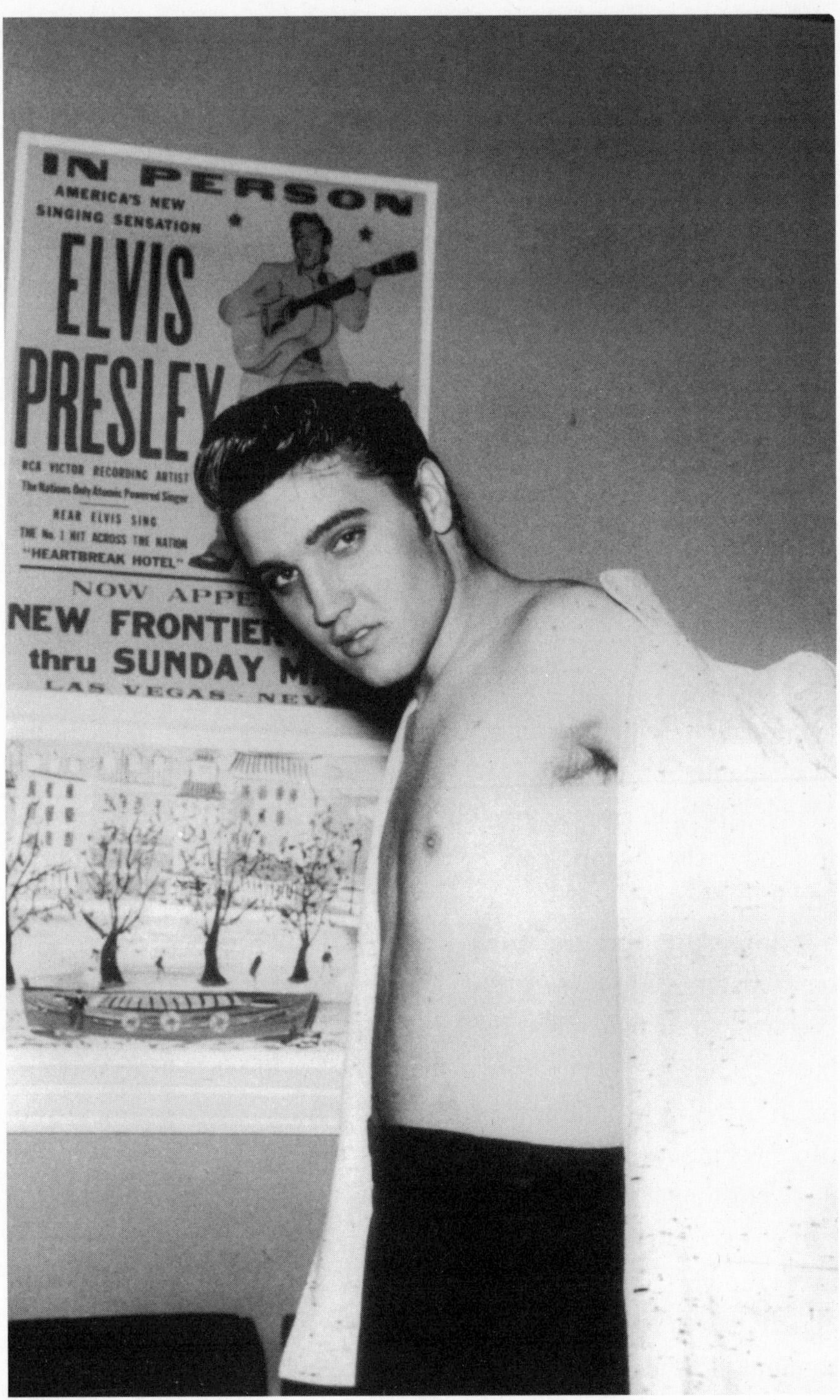
IN PERSON
AMERICA'S NEW
SINGING SENSATION
ELVIS
PRESLEY
RCA VICTOR RECORDING ARTIST
The Nations Only Atomic Powered Singer
HEAR ELVIS SING
THE No. 1 HIT ACROSS THE NATION
"HEARTBREAK HOTEL"
NOW APPE
NEW FRONTIE
thru SUNDAY M
LAS VEGAS NEV

much controversy when it was released in the mid '50s. Elvis and the band maintain a clean, fast pace, but this rendition is performed too carefully and predictably. Elvis sings "oooo" hesitantly, almost as if he can hear Little Richard in his head, and for one of the few times in his career, seems slightly intimidated. However, Elvis's version is definitely superior to Pat Boone's homogenized pop smash, which sounds much like Wayne Newton would if he were to attempt James Brown's "Sex Machine."

"Tutti Frutti, good booty"—bolt the door, Grandma, Little Richard is prowlin' the neighborhood.

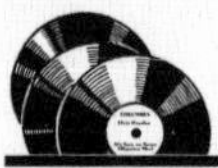

Money Honey *(Elvis Presley, 1956)*

The original studio recording (1956) is good but lacks the proper balance between concept and presentation. On the *Elvis—The Greatest Performances* television broadcast, Priscilla Presley introduces the most memorable live television performance of this song—Elvis's March 24, 1956, appearance on *The Dorsey Brothers Stage Show*—at the end of the documentary by commenting that Elvis "was still raw and full of energy." That's the secret here. The song is stripped down; the final verse from the original ("Well, I learned a lesson . . .") is omitted, and verse three ". . . Tell me, baby, what's wrong with you") becomes verse two, tightening the song's focus. The instrumental break technically occurs in the same place (after verse two) but fits much better now, coming shortly after the song's toughest line: "from this day on our romance is through."

This break is a joy to behold, with Elvis's rhythm guitar mixed very loud, Scotty Moore sniping off lead notes, D. J. Fontana bouncing behind his drum kit, and Bill Black releasing both hands from his upright bass at one point and shaking them above his shoulders. Elvis shimmies low and sultrily, mugging superbly to the camera throughout. His eyes look dazed as he sings the opening lines about the landlord, then suddenly gaze upward on the "uh hoo hoo" refrain after the "tell me baby, face to face" verse, hoping for money to come falling from the sky. The hiccuping delivery is never overdone and hits just the right spots, as on the first two words of "Ho-ow co-uld another man take my place?"

Too Much *(Elvis: Worldwide 50 Gold Award Hits, Vol. 1, 1970)*

This may be the worst-written song Elvis ever turned into a fine record. On paper, this is a nothing song, but Elvis's performance, the production, the overall sound, and the musicians—especially Scotty Moore—turn it into a worthwhile rocker. Elvis sings with a steady intensity, effectively pulling listeners into the song.

Released in 1957, "Too Much" is an unjustly neglected record, showcasing the legendary band with no name. Scotty Moore's guitar solo after Elvis's plea ("Don't you leave me broken-hearted . . ."), heralded by D. J. Fontana's drums, defines low-register technique.

"Too Much" is a fine example of syncopated . . . ah . . . harmony between Elvis, the musicians, and the Jordanaires—so sophisticated and sleek, yet planting firmly once again the roots of rock 'n' roll. It's also a primer of late '50s vocabulary: "too much," "flip-flip," "you're the most," "treatin' your daddy wrong."

Elvis's voice breaks once: "I'm such a fool for ah your charms, take me back ah baby in your arms." On "take," where the word splits in half, Elvis captures the essence of high school romance, like a schoolboy asking "Runaround Sue" for another date, half cocky, half ready to bolt back to the football field with the guys. The leather jacket and the famous cuddly sneer are back for one more try ("I need ah your huggin', please be mine"). Then the finale ("cause I love you too much") stops the song dead in its tracks, "much" echoing like the kick start of a motorcycle whose rider is unaware that his sweetheart is watching from a distance, in loving silence.

All Shook Up *(Elvis: Worldwide 50 Gold Award Hits, Vol. 1, 1970)*

Many experts, including Paul McCartney and Elton John, consider this to be one of the King's finest records. The rhythm section hums like a blown-out transformer on a utility pole, one line down, flashing sparks on the sidewalk. It's a simmering, stir-fry sound, and Elvis's voice ("a volcano that's hot"), is full of crackles and pops, as if it's ready to burst into flames. But it never does, and that's why "All Shook Up" is such a great recording.

Elvis is the master chef, cooking up a storm without burning the recipe ("My heart beats so, it scares me to death"). The syncopated percussion beat is the paramedics rapping on your door. It's too late, and all the neighbors are wondering what's going on. As Greil Marcus points out, Elvis's "throaty nuances" are a highlight, such as when he sings "I'm proud to say that she's my buttercup" with absolutely no sense of possessiveness.

For those who did not experience the phenomenon, it is very difficult to imagine just how popular Elvis Presley was in the 1950s. The only parallel was Beatlemania. The youth of America found their generational hero—and everything was Elvis. There were Elvis sheets, hairbrushes, stuffed hound dogs, T-shirts, bubble gum, ball-point pens, stickpins, hood ornaments, and most anything else one could imagine. There were thousands of Elvis Presley fan clubs throughout the world, and the King received 20,000 adoring letters a week. Whatever Elvis did attracted attention, and he became an instant event, constantly breaking attendance and viewership records.

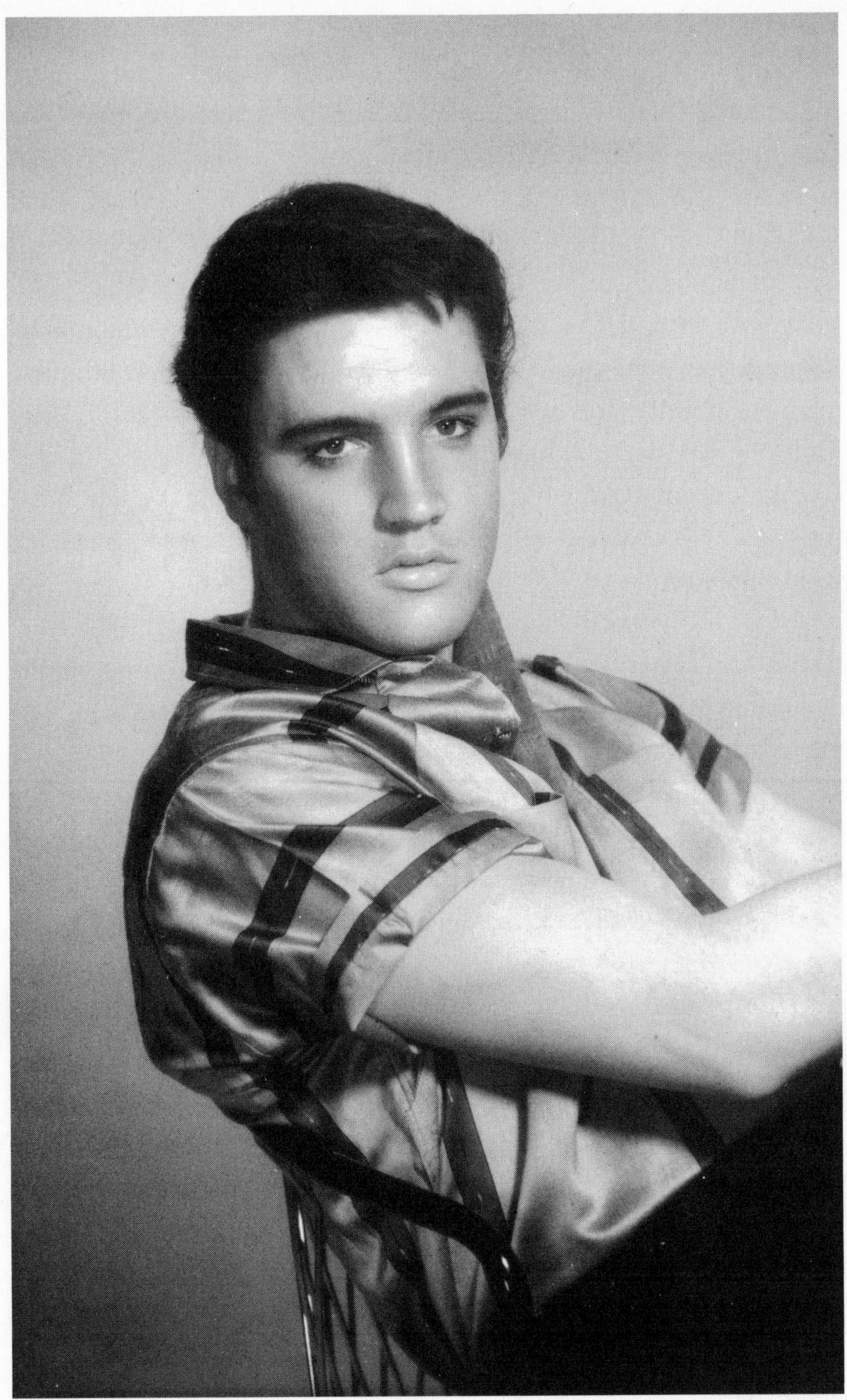

For example, the first time Elvis appeared on *The Ed Sullivan Show*, the program attracted a staggering 82.6 percent of the national viewing audience! The Beatles never equaled that *percentage* of viewers. Elvis also performed at football stadiums—unheard of at the time—and pulled capacity crowds.

Elvis was in tune with the times, knew who was making great new music and who wasn't, and was just as adept at divining popular culture's heartbeat. For instance, it took only one jam session with Jerry Lee Lewis for the King to know that "the Killer" was uniquely talented. Unlike later years, when he would withdraw behind the walls of Graceland and have no inkling of what was happening, this young Elvis was making things happen. The black hair, the sideburns, the sneer, the shocking music, all became the radical prototype for youthful imitation.

Due to this social impact—which had a lot to do with sex—establishment critics were vicious toward Elvis. Most of the criticism was directed at his suggestive pelvic thrusts, particularly the ones he exhibited while performing "Hound Dog" on *The Milton Berle Show*. Jack O'Brien of the *New York Journal American* spouted: "[Elvis] makes up for vocal shortcomings with the weirdest and plainly planned, suggestive animation short of aborigines' mating dances." This was clearly a racist comment—and it was directed toward a white man!

New York Times writer Jack Gould warned: "When Presley executes his bumps and grinds, it must be remembered by the Columbia Broadcasting System that even a 12-year-old's curiosity may be overstimulated."

Notre Dame prohibited its students from attending Elvis concerts. In fact, such bans were issued in many parts of the country at high schools, colleges, and other institutions. Many school officials prohibited students from dressing or looking like Elvis, whose effigy was hung in Nashville and burned to cinders in St. Louis. A disk jockey in Nashville torched Elvis's records in a local park.

But despite such extreme reactions, Elvis remained the King of the heap. And performers such as Chuck Berry, Little Richard, Jerry Lee Lewis, Otis Blackwell, Bill Haley, and others were envious of both his musical success and the public attention showered on him.

Love Me Tender (*Elvis: Worldwide 50 Gold Award Hits, Vol. 1*, 1970)

Elvis's voice is dark and brooding, intimate as candlelight. The acoustic guitar chords are soft as a woman's ribs, and Elvis sings to the whole woman: lullaby, seduction, reverence, respect. He holds back gently, her voice in his heart, the texture and tenor of the words rich as an anniversary feast of double Chateaubriand.

Yet maybe it's a dream—the listener doesn't really know if the couple is together or apart. "All my dreams fulfilled" is thus a paradox, split between yearning and satisfaction. Grammatically, "tender" should be "tenderly" (also rhymes with "me"). But for Elvis, "Tender" is her name, her whole being, much more than an adverb depicting how something should be done. "Tender" also means "an offer of money or service in payment of an obligation" and "a vessel attendant on another vessel . . . One that ferries supplies between ship and shore." "Legal Tender." Or is it illegal? Elvis always injected multiple, subtle shades of meaning into his songs. Is this woman an angel or a prostitute?

Either way, does it really make any difference? As John Fiske says in his essay "Madonna," regarding "Like a Virgin" and the line "Touched for the very first time": "Touched . . . has religious meanings of 'laying on of hands' . . . physical ones of sexuality, emotional ones of true love, and streetwise ones of near madness and loss of control."

Elvis treads the line between chauvinism and enlightenment very delicately here. Yes, "Love Me Tender" aches with its simplicity. Jack Scott's "Young Love" mines the same vein ("Filled with true devotion . . . shared with deep emotion!"). "Young Love" was a contemporary hit, and deservedly so, but it can't touch "Love Me Tender," an unforgettably close encounter.

Teddy Bear and **Good Luck Charm** *(Elvis: Worldwide 50 Gold Award Hits, Vol. 1,* 1970)

Would it be a sin to suggest that Elvis invented bubblegum music? (Remember his wonderful laugh from the live, out-of-control "Are You Lonesome Tonight?") These two songs are together because they reflect the perfect young adolescent date of the now-lost innocent '50s. Thirteen-year-old Elvis (Teddy) and 12-year-old Stacy (Charm) are in the front row of the Ritz Theater, watching *Fantasia*. Their parents dropped them off, promising to be back at four. Instead, the youngsters wait for two hours in the parking lot, eating sandwiches, drinking Cokes, singing Elvis tunes out loud (there is no car radio). A patrol car cruises by.

In the mid- to late 1960s the Archies ("Sugar, Sugar" may be the quintessential bubblegum song) and Tommy James ("I Think We're Alone Now," more sophisticated Double Bubble, as was Herman's Hermits' "Mrs. Brown") exemplified what was thought to be a new genre. "Yummy Yummy" (Ohio Express) is an incredible song for two reasons. First, like the others, it desperately tried to recreate—yet mock—that giddy, easy '50s feeling of young flirtation (the couple in the front row at the Ritz brushes hands only once, thrillingly). Second, it is totally unlike the other '60s songs mentioned here because the raspy vocals and frenetic musical pace give it an edge much like Johnny Rotten and the Sex Pistols would achieve a decade later. This is Bazooka Bubblegum.

The point here is that bubblegum music was an attempt to either imitate or satirize what Elvis accomplished with "Teddy Bear" and "Good Luck Charm." "Sugar Sugar," although not to the extent of "Yummy Yummy" or Motown's soap-bubble entry "Jimmy Mack," is also a humorous jibe at the '50s. Don't forget—these songs were released during the era of "19th Nervous Breakdown," "Helter Skelter," and napalm strikes in Vietnam.

These two Elvis tunes are not just premature, corner drugstore rings around Teddy and Stacy's fingers. If you listen closely, Elvis takes a humorous look at the already too idealized '50s notion of adolescent love. The Monotones' "Book of Love" is a great example of this, too. Yet Elvis not only plays with the songs, he creates the innocent identity, something the Toys were able to recreate on their 1965 hit "Lovers' Concerto."

There is still another dimension here, however. Elvis sings with coy passion ("Oh oh oh Teddy Bear"), but there are sinister flashes in his eyes that say "you ain't seen nothin' yet," like Woody Harrelson in *Natural Born Killers*. The bubblegum cracks. Are these songs sexist? Maybe a little ("Lions play too rough"). Let's cue up Bobby Rydell's "Wild One." That's cool. And lame. "Be wild about me!"

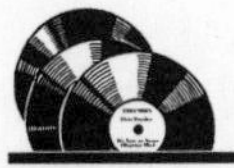

When My Blue Moon Turns to Gold Again

(*Elvis*, 1957)

This mediocre song is made irresistible by Elvis, his feel for music splashing a rainbow in the sky. The Jordanaires shine as they sing like kids on a Brooklyn street corner after school has been dismissed early—vibrant and buoyant in their unexpected freedom—especially in the near falsetto ending that parodies the Dubs' 1957 release "Don't Ask Me to Be Lonely."

It doesn't matter which song came first. "Blue Moon/Gold" is doo-wop with a difference; it's so joyful and reaffirming, yet Elvis's vocal injects a touch of melancholy. Listen to it again, and there are bits and pieces of the blues, as in the final "back within my arms to stay," sung with glimpses of doubt. Elvis is the Great Pretender.

Ready Teddy *(Elvis, 1957)*

Little Richard's version of "Ready Teddy" is arguably his finest record, but Elvis comes close to creating the same frenzy here. He really rocks and inspires the band to deliver driving, wild, gutty rock 'n' roll. "Ready ready ready to rock 'n' roll" is delivered like a battle cry, punctuated by drums that urge the charge.

The main reason we have selected "Ready Teddy" as one of Elvis's most significant songs is because it offers further proof that the King's best performances go beyond just his greatest hits. Here, Elvis rocks with energy, daring, and drive, motivating those around him to achieve a higher level of creativity. It is one of his most exciting performances.

Blue Suede Shoes *(Elvis Presley, 1956)*

Carl Perkins wrote this classic and was the first to record it as a rockabilly song, but Elvis saw much more in "Blue Suede Shoes." It's not that Perkins didn't sense the potential social dynamite in his song; he did, and he was afraid of it. Even after his rockabilly version was released, Perkins retreated from the song. He released other records that were further withdrawals from the threatening lyrics of "Blue Suede Shoes." But even if Perkins hadn't feared the outcry this song might evoke, he did not possess the fire, energy, or scope that Elvis did. It should be noted that Carl Perkins was one of many singers who were consciously working to synthesize a new sound from diverse musical elements before Elvis.

Perkins was a talented musician and an excellent guitarist, but this was a song Elvis had to record, because it defined him so perfectly. Elvis may be singing the same lyrics as Perkins on "Blue Suede Shoes," but he is by no means performing the same song. Elvis and his band turn this nice little song that means no harm to anyone into a vehicle of overt protest and arrogant defiance. As the saying goes, It's not what you say, it's how you say it.

Elvis stakes a claim here, declaring that these Blue Suede Shoes are his property alone. It's as if he is saying, "Don't tread on me. I'll go anywhere I want in these shoes, and do what I please. Nobody is going to stop me."

Although the contentious lyrics may have suggested otherwise, Elvis still waited to release "Blue Suede Shoes" until after Perkins had a hit with it. His performance of "Hound Dog" on *The Milton Berle Show* and his recordings of "Hound Dog" and "Blue Suede Shoes" prove that the King knew what he was doing, and that he also desired the public reaction the songs were engendering. Jerry Schilling, Elvis's most knowledgeable friend, verified this. As only a shrewd revolutionary would know, Elvis *had* to perform "Blue Suede Shoes." It was critical to the social revolution he was implementing.

With all due deference to Carl Perkins, "Blue Suede Shoes" didn't become the rage until Elvis danced in them.

♦ ♦ ♦ ♦

According to friend Eddie Fidal, personal testimonies from ladies involved, and also TV interviews, Elvis saw a *lot* of young women—girls around 15 years of age. But what is not realized by many biographers is that Elvis didn't have sex with these underage stargazers. He may have entertained several at a time and actually had more than a few in his bed at once, but he didn't have sexual intercourse with them. The big caveat is that, while this behavior seems to have been essentially innocent, it was very misguided, betraying major flaws in Elvis's understanding of women and sex.

He did have sex with other women more his own age, but Elvis was a highly sexed person, and the conflict with that sexuality spurred the fever of his performances.

As Fidal relates, the one girl Elvis probably saw the most during the 1950s was Anita Wood, a blonde who aspired to be a singer. A bootleg tape captures Wood, Elvis, Fidal, and Fidal's family sitting around the piano, discussing music and Ms. Wood's future. Elvis wanted the young woman to sing some gutty numbers, like Connie Francis, even though the King didn't like all of Connie's work, implying that some of it was too syrupy.

Eventually, Elvis saw less and less of Anita, and by the time he was inducted into the Army, their relationship was over.

Except for not getting enough sleep and worrying about his mother's deteriorating health (which didn't yet appear to be too serious), Elvis was still exhilarated, although confused. Having gone through such a whirlwind of hysterical popularity in so short a time was a great strain. Indeed, instant fame has slain many mercurial players, from James Dean to Kurt Cobain. Even Paul Newman, who has handled the spotlight admirably for decades, said that if stardom had been thrust upon him abruptly, rather than gradually, it was unlikely that he could have handled it. The young Elvis Presley was very strong and level-headed, but even so, there were indications that he was beginning to veer toward disaster.

At this point in his career, Elvis was not a very sophisticated man, so the women he chose to be with were not usually big-name bombshells, according to a variety of sources. One major exception was Natalie Wood, who threw herself at the King like an eager starlet. When

Elvis matured, many women praised him as a lover, but Natalie Wood was completely turned off. She was used to Hollywood/New York-style encounters, perhaps a tryst at the Beverly Hilton or the Ritz, while Elvis was more familiar with high school romance. He gave her a ride on his motorcycle and took her to an amusement park, and his friends often hung around while the couple was dating. By most accounts, Elvis was not ready for sex after a single date, but according to Joe Esposito, Elvis's road manager, Natalie definitely was.

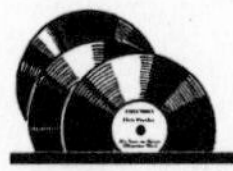

Rip It Up (*Elvis*, 1957)

This is one of the best cuts on Elvis's second album. The production is tight and tough, and Elvis's voice is almost desperately confident. The song begins with D. J. Fontana popping out a rhythm that's akin to nervously tapping a pencil on a table—he just can't wait to get going. Elvis opens up suddenly: "It's Saturday night and I just got paid" (chord), "fooling around money I don't try to save" (chord). The chords at the end of each line serve as exclamation points. There is a continuing theme of the musical interplay between Elvis's singing and the musical backup. Each vocal, musical line, and punctuation propels the wild purpose. This is the essence of the album.

Listen to the fusion in the chorus: "I'm going to rip it up" (cadence), "I'm gonna rock it up" (cadence), I'm going to shake it up" (cadence), "I'm going to rip it up." Only the drumming is constant. To maintain the structural coherence while avoiding redundancy, there is a crazy, loose, lewd guitar solo. Scotty Moore sounds like he is jamming musical charts through a paper shredder as he pushes his guitar to sustain the wired, magical energy while the band careens along, almost out of control.

Elvis's performance oozes excitement. This is X-rated stuff as the King sings "ball it up" just as Little Richard did. However, Elvis's version of "Rip It Up" incites more anticipation than Little Richard's rendition. Richard sings full blast from the beginning to the end of the song, but Elvis creates a sense of wonder—and is more diverse. While Richard uses the saxophone as the main instrument, Elvis wisely weaves together different instruments—drums, piano, guitar. The instrumental part of Elvis's recording, led by Moore's fiery lead guitar and Fontana's furious drumming, is more dominant than Little Richard's sax-lead break.

We're not saying that Elvis performs this song better than Little Richard—after all, it's Little Richard at his best. According to Greil Marcus, the young Richard could "lift the words off the page." But the fact that Elvis could sing a Little Richard song so well is a testament to his musical ability.

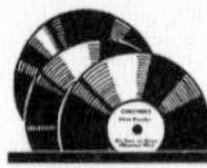

Long Tall Sally (*Elvis*, 1957)

Elvis's cover versions of songs initially recorded by black artists, such as "Blue Moon," "That's All Right (Mama)," and "Long Tall Sally," are performed straight out, with reverence to the originals. But with "Long Tall Sally," he pulls back the passion a little bit, almost questioning, like a kid going to another Saturday night party with his buddies and wondering why they are doing it. They're "gonna have some fun tonight," but maybe everything isn't all right, after all. Maybe there's going to be some trouble, a little confusion about personal identity.

It is this interpretive distinction that makes any discussion about Elvis ripping off black artists—or anyone else—unfair and distorting. Little Richard's version of "Long Tall Sally" reigns supreme, yet Elvis makes us think about the reverberations of wildness in meaningful ways.

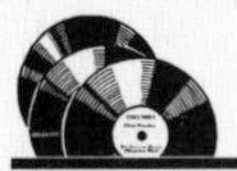

Jailhouse Rock (*Elvis: Worldwide 50 Gold Award Hits, Vol. I*, 1970)

Just when it appeared that Elvis couldn't expand the horizons of rock music any further, he delivered perhaps his greatest performance of the 1950s with this song.

Jarring the listener like a burglar smashing a door latch with what has become one of the most familiar openings in rock 'n' roll, "Jailhouse Rock" epitomizes the genre. D. J. Fontana's drums slam like a pile driver against Dudley Moore's rollicking roadhouse piano, while Bill Black's bass skillfully weaves the sounds together. In what might rightly be called the invention of power chording, Scotty Moore drives his guitar to reflect Elvis's intensity.

Elvis's singing takes us into uncharted territory. This song elicits movement, quivers at the edges of a riot. What comes through is a barking, snapping, violent explosion that commands the audience to action.

"Jailhouse Rock" and "Hound Dog" were the foundation of much of the hard rock genre that would follow. For instance, listen to "Jailhouse Rock," then immediately play Bruce Springsteen's "Born in the U.S.A." Although this Springsteen single is one of the most galvanizing hard rock songs ever recorded, the influence of "Jailhouse Rock" is unmistakable.

"Jailhouse Rock" lit a blowtorch to the musical synergy of the early Elvis era, but it was also the last record of that epoch. Elvis would continue to make great recordings that scanned the radar screens of rock 'n' roll and popular culture, but the revolutionary part of his career was over. Nevertheless, as confirmed by most rock authorities, Elvis Presley revolutionized music and culture.

What did Elvis crystalize during those four years, 1954 through 1957? The first *Rolling Stone Record Guide* says it best: "Suffice it to say that these records, more than any others, contain the seeds of everything rock 'n' roll was, has been, and most likely what it may foreseeably become." The landmark recordings include all of the rock 'n' roll cuts on *The Complete Sun Sessions*, the first two RCA albums, and many of the great singles discussed here.

(You're So Square) Baby, I Don't Care (*Elvis: The Other Sides; Worldwide Gold Award Hits, Vol. 2,* 1971)

Elvis's vocal on "Baby, I Don't Care" sounds like he's singing through the take-out microphone at Wendy's. It's so cool; the feel is like fries and Frosties in the back parking lot. You can almost see the rebel with his middle-class suburban girl in a battered, once-repossessed '56 Olds Rocket 88 as Elvis pants "care, care, care." Hot chili to go.

Although this is a well-written song by Mike Leiber and Jerry Stoller, there were nonetheless problems in the studio. Bill Black could not get the bass line right, so Elvis Presley himself played bass and achieved a jumbled, thrusting, teenage make-out sound. The feel and magic added to this song by the King are heavenly.

"You don't like hotrod racin'," Elvis sings, bewildered by his girl. Now they're watching every heat together at the local track. This song is a veritable seminar on concise rock 'n' roll.

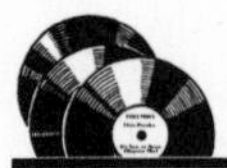

I Beg of You (*Essential Elvis, Vol. 2,* 1988, and *Elvis: Worldwide 50 Gold Award Hits, Vol. 1,* 1970)

Few realize the extent of Elvis's contributions to the studio singles and albums he recorded throughout his career. He was as adept at innovation in the studio as he was on stage. A perfect example is the painstaking and meticulous production of 1957's superb yet often forgotten "I Beg of You." We listened to four out of twentysomething run-throughs of the song, and it is clear that Elvis was in charge of this production. At the end of one take, he seems to be dissatisfied with the instrumentation and the Jordanaires' too-high, harsh, out-of-rhythm backup vocals, and says, "We're gonna fade out at the end." That Elvis was asserting his authority is evident, when one listens to the other takes from the session, as the song gradually discovers its infectious personality.

Previous takes of "Beg" focus too much on the lead guitar and drums—especially a banging bass drum—and Elvis's voice is lost in the logjam. The guitar seems out of synch at times, as do the Jordanaires' backing vocals, which often overpower Elvis's articulation and struggling intonations. He is singing from the bottom of a wishing well, trying to be heard over the splashing of coins being thrown into the water.

The final rendition, however, yields an accomplished rock song. The twanging, overpowering lead guitar is gone, replaced by soft fills. The drums provide a smooth underpinning, and the Jordanaires' "ah ah ooos" now urgently complement Elvis's "Darlin', please please love me too, I beg of you." When he sings, "Hold my hand and promise that you'll always love me too," Elvis growls "Hold" like a hungry rottweiler, then finishes the line almost as smoothly as Bessie Smith at her best. The song fades out sweetly with "Please please love me too" repeated three times.

It is interesting to note that certain stylings in this song can also be found in other artists' recordings. For instance, the repeated "please" is the cornerstone of the Beatles' "Please Please Me," and a revised "Please please love me too" is evident in their hit "Love Me Do." James Brown screamed "Please Please Please" onto the r&b charts in 1956, and Chuck Berry employed the repeated-word motif as he chanted "Hail, hail rock 'n' roll." These artists and their music touch one another in intriguing ways that may never be fully understood.

Essential Elvis, Vol. 2 offers three different takes of "I Beg of You," but *Elvis: Worldwide 50 Gold Award Hits, Vol. 1* includes the final and best performance.

Trouble (*King Creole,* 1958)

"Go ahead, make my day." That classic but much overused Clint Eastwood line from the Dirty Harry movie *Sudden Impact* fits this song perfectly. Play the entire Elvis catalog, including all of your bootlegs, and you won't hear a song as bizarre as "Trouble," from the 1958 *King Creole* soundtrack.

The lines "I was born standin' up and talkin' back" and "don't take no orders from no kind of man" embody the marking of territory that is instinctive among young males: James Dean's knife fight in *Rebel Without a Cause*, the Sharks and Jets in *West Side Story,* the drug dealers in *New Jack City*. "Trouble" also signals animosity between generations: "My daddy was a green-eyed mountain jack / because I'm evil, my middle name is misery." Like father, like son? Maybe, but in Shakespeare's *Othello*, "the green-eyed monster" was the enemy "jealousy," a fatal flaw.

Here, "Trouble" is a double bourbon with a dash of Cajun hot sauce for satire. The melody and vocal style recall Peggy Lee's "I'm a Woman," gettin' grits ready to challenge all comers, especially if her man wants to criticize. Elvis sings, "If you're gonna start a rumble, don't you try it all alone." Are we in the kitchen during a domestic dispute? Are we in a back alley, down by the docks, with chains dragging across the cement, sirens wailing, ships' horns blowing (maybe John Coltrane sat in for this session)?

That works, but actually we're in a strip joint here, the raunchy, muffled horn flowing up a lazy river for Gypsy Rose Lee, Filly Corral, Mississippi Queen. It's New Orleans lounge blues, fake Delta Muddy

Waters. Elvis intones, "Well, I'm evil, so don't you mess around . . ." as drums thunder like an old Peterbilt semi trying to start at the roadside cafe. Now for the *really* bizarre stuff: The song breaks into Dixieland! Preservation Hall would be proud. Elvis's voice picks up the tempo: "I'm evil, evil as can be," and "Trouble" crashes into Broadway musical excessiveness at the end—complete with cowbells!

What happened to the rebel? He's in a Hollywood movie. *King Creole* is one of Elvis's best, but there are few of this caliber. "Trouble," as perplexing as it is, demonstrates some of the diversity and range of Elvis's talent.

Finally, the rebel must have gotten through to somebody. Remember Janis Joplin's "Turtle Blues" from *Cheap Thrills*? "They call me mean, they call me evil . . . Ain't nobody gonna dog me down." That song has the same sleazy bar feel of "Trouble," and it's one of Janis's most endearing numbers.

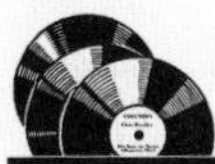

One Night of Sin *(Reconsider Baby, 1985)*

This is Elvis's version of the Smiley Lewis original, and it couldn't pass the censors, so the King substantially altered the song, cleaning it up and turning it into the 1958 love story "One Night with You." In "One Night of Sin" Elvis sings, "that very quiet life has caused me nothin' but harm." In "One Night with You," he changes that vision of guilt and remorse to pure supplication: "Now I know that life without you has been too lonely too long." "What I'm now paying for" becomes "What I'm now *praying* for"—making the song mainstream. "One Night with You," released in 1958, is a good, strong blues-rock number, but it is utterly transformed in 1968 at Elvis's Burbank concerts, as discussed later in this book.

"One Night of Sin" is much closer to Robert Johnson's brand of confessional blues, heavy with anguish and unresolved conflicts ("I lost my sweet helpin' hand, I got myself to blame"). One can almost hear Elvis tiptoeing past the church on his way to the harlot's house, hell-hounds on his trail. The opening notes of the song recall the intro to the Platters' 1955 hit, "The Great Pretender," but Elvis is not pretending here ("Don't call my name, it makes me feel so ashamed"). The musical contrast is eerily effective in helping to communicate the essence of the singer's feelings: A broken heart hurts, but losing one's soul in the process is like being stranded in a howling wind, far from a lover's door and forgiveness, which is what Elvis evokes here.

As noted previously, Greil Marcus has observed that Elvis's genius was his ability to take the guilt out of the blues and still make the music ring true. On "One Night of Sin," Elvis is loaded with guilt, proving that he can sing the blues either way and still make it authentic.

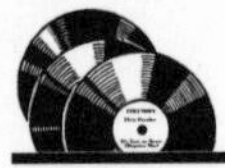

I Need Your Love Tonight (*Elvis: The Other Sides; Worldwide Gold Award Hits, Vol. 2,* 1971)

Listen to the way Elvis flirts with the words like the new kid in school doing card tricks to catch the attention of the prettiest girl in class. He's slick and debonair, full of innocent mischief. When he scats "ooee . . . ooo wow," a kind of devilish persona emerges—sexy and powerful, yet with a boyish sense of humor about romance. "I can't let you go" is both gentle and lusty in its delivery.

Elvis's conscription into the armed forces in 1958 saddened ardent fans, but both supporters and critics reacted with pride and respect at his calm and mature acceptance of military duty. In fact, the King won many new followers by tempering rebelliousness with a traditional sense of social responsibility.

CHAPTER 3

The Sixties: Return of the Thunderbird/Lost in the Maze

There are a few significant points that should be made about Elvis's two years in the Army. He did not contest going into the military and, most importantly, he was a model soldier, according to numerous sources. Practically everyone who served with him has said that Elvis never asked for special privileges and was just a regular G.I. However, as Red West and Sonny West, Elvis's personal bodyguards and members of the so-called "Memphis Mafia," have testified, the King did not want to be drafted. Eddie Fidal corroborated this story to us. And, as many others believe, he also thought that the government engineered his conscription to destroy his career and drive a stake into his influence on the youth of America.

It was in the army that Elvis first learned about the temptations of amphetamines. He indulged when he was on night duty, so that he wouldn't fall asleep. This was not an uncommon practice among inductees, but in retrospect, perhaps it was the first warning sign of what would later become his battle with prescription drugs.

Elvis's popularity at the time was so great that, when he was assigned to overseas duty, he found it impossible to eat in German restaurants because he was inundated by enthusiastic fans. During a leave in Paris, however, he did manage to frequent at least one restaurant surreptitiously.

It was in Germany that Elvis met his future wife, Priscilla Beaulieu. His road manager and friend, Joe Esposito, related firsthand that it was love at first sight, one of those rare instances when the chemistry between two people was so powerful that it made each feel like swinging joyfully from a chandelier.

The apparent ploy by the United States government to ruin Elvis Presley by inducting him into military service seemed not only to have failed, but when Elvis had completed his tour of duty, his popularity upon his return to the States was at least as great as it had ever been. However, Uncle Sam and the army succeeded in one major way: They took most of the rebelliousness out of Elvis, who, unlike most entertainment rebels, had been a real threat to the status quo.

From the federal government to the late author Albert Goldman and others, there have been numerous attempts to discredit Elvis Presley. The desire to silence him is as strong today as it ever was. However, Elvis Presley's legacy has always survived the paranoia and disgust of corporate America—even while it continues to exploit his legend. Today, Elvis has been sanitized into a near-perfect being, yet he is also trivialized on talk shows—the butt of usually tasteless jokes.

It should be remembered that the extent of ridicule often disguises petty jealousy and a very disturbing inability to cherish greatness. Sadly, it seems that if we have not achieved greatness ourselves, Americans are inclined to extinguish its light whenever it shines in our eyes. Undeniably, Elvis did generate his own demise, but while Americans tend to scavenge the fallen—or even precipitate their plunge from glory—it is a testament to our reverence for rebelliousness that we continue to revere Elvis as a hero. This dichotomy is an unsolvable puzzle.

Throughout his hitch in the army, Elvis remained the monarch of rock 'n' roll. However, the cast of characters had changed, and many of the great rockers were gone. Little Richard had entered the seminary, Jerry Lee Lewis was banned from the public, and Buddy Holly was dead. By the time Elvis returned to civilian life, the top-selling recording artists (besides himself) were Rick Nelson, Connie Francis, Bobby Darin, Frankie Avalon, Fabian, and Sam Cooke. Although a few of these performers—such as Cooke, Nelson, and, to a lesser degree, Francis and Darin—did some memorable work, many critics believed that rock's first golden era was over.

Elvis's first comeback single, "Stuck On You," went to number one on the charts, and when he appeared on the lowly ranked *Frank Sinatra Show,* the program's ratings went through the roof as the audience screamed at everything he did on stage. There were thousands of Elvis Presley fan clubs around the world with hundreds of thousands of members, and the star continued to receive 20,000 letters a week.

According to Eddie Fidal, Elvis was feeling rejuvenated upon his return from the army, despite the loss of his mother, Gladys, who had died while he was in the service. Although he would never completely recover from her death, he could at least accept the fact of her passing.

The most important mind-set Elvis had was that he was a gifted artist who wanted to make great music. Bruce Springsteen once said of the King, "Elvis was an artist, and he was into *being* an artist." That statement rang particularly true in the mid-1950s, upon his return from the army, and when he made his great comeback in 1968–69.

Elvis had new ideas about the kind of music he wanted to record and different conceptions concerning the sound he wanted to achieve. This led to one of his finest recording sessions, which yielded the 1960 hit album *Elvis Is Back.*

♦ ♦ ♦ ♦

Fame and Fortune *(Elvis: The Other Sides; Worldwide Gold Award Hits, Vol. 2,* 1971)

"Fame and Fortune" (1960) was released at a critical juncture in Elvis's career: his first "comeback" following military service and preceding the endless cycle of mostly mediocre musical films. This song anticipates many of the professional and personal doldrums which would follow ("Fame and fortune, how empty they can beee") yet also serves notice that, at some level, Elvis always knew what was really important ("but when I hold you in my arms, that's a heaven to meee"). The way he enunciates and draws out the word "touch" ("Ah, but the *touch* of your lips on mine makes me feel like a king") recalls the delicacy of his delivery on "Love Me Tender" years before. It may be even more profound here, because the listener can sense his awareness of the tenuous balance between fulfillment and emptiness.

The musical intro is quite reminiscent of the Shields' 1958 hit, "You Cheated," while the repeated "wanu wah ooh" backup vocals call to mind the Fleetwoods' fabulous "Mr. Blue" of 1959. The combination of these sounds and Elvis's own doo-wop original, "woe do dume," before "to know you love me brings fame and fortune my way," is delicate and memorable. Subtle and sleek guitar, piano pricking like budding roses, and bass and drums creeping like spring roots enhance this pivotal performance in Elvis's catalogue.

Upon Elvis's return from the army, he essentially reformed the band, while searching for a different sound. He now had two guitarists, Scotty Moore and Hank Garland, and two drummers, D. J. Fontana and Buddy Harman. Bill Black was replaced by Bob Moore

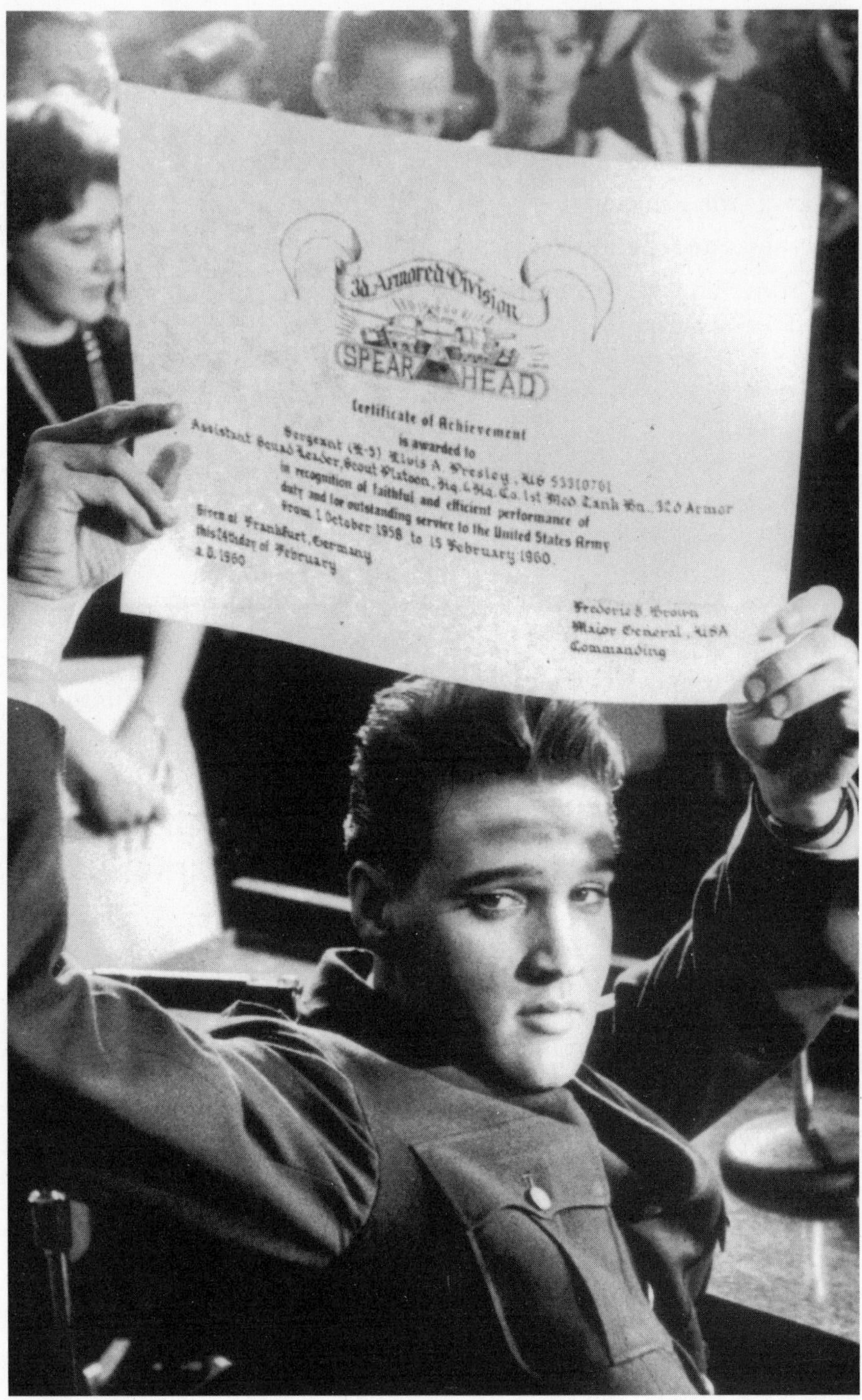
3d Armored Division
SPEAR HEAD
Certificate of Achievement
is awarded to
Sergeant (E-5) Elvis A. Presley, US 53310761
Assistant Squad Leader, Scout Platoon, Hq. & Hq. Co. 1st Med Tank Bn., 32d Armor
in recognition of faithful and efficient performance of
duty and for outstanding service to the United States Army
from 1 October 1958 to 15 February 1960.
Given at Frankfurt, Germany
this 24th day of February
A.D. 1960
Frederic J. Brown
Major General, USA
Commanding

on bass. Most importantly, Elvis brought in one of the greatest saxophone players ever, Homer "Boots" Randolph. The Jordanaires remained for awhile.

The new ensemble was exploring its range on the following tracks, as the King cut one of his most brilliant albums, *Elvis Is Back*, which features the most evocative blues performances of his career. The songs analyzed in the following section of this chapter can be found on that album, cassette, or CD.

♦ ♦ ♦ ♦

Make Me Know It

This is the first cut on an album that improves with every listening. "Make Me Know It" is a jaunty, swinging tune, full of life and optimism ("If you care, come over here . . . make me know you do"). The youthful vitality of dalliance is devoid of threat or complication ("You say you've got kisses. . . . Come right along, you'll find me helpful as can be"). It's astonishing to hear the dark "Reconsider Baby" at the end of the album and remember the bright and fresh innocence that opens this eclectic collection. It's like hearing "A Day in the Life" from *Sergeant Pepper* and then recalling the album's upbeat title cut.

On "Make Me Know It," Elvis's voice is as smooth as a leather jacket that's been worn for years, supple in the elbows and shoulders, snug around the waist like a woman's arm. The piano chords and bass lines that bridge the verses are tight and succinct.

The last time we saw this couple they were waiting in line to ride the Tilt-A-Whirl, munching a cloud of pink cotton candy, stealing kisses between bites.

Fever

When Peggy Lee sang "Fever" in 1958, she created a huge sensation, her voice daring yet restrained, lonesome, skirting the edge, barely, softly, of female aggression. Whispering hints of despair, as in her later "Is That All There Is?" she's singing into a mirror, mascara skid marks on her cheeks, yet she's somehow fully in charge.

Enter Elvis with this song that can be interpreted as a response to Peggy's plea in her own "Fever." Bold, seductive, irresistible—the finger-poppin', knuckle-crackin', soft heartbeat bass line of the intro is Elvis rapping on her door as he sings "Never knew how much I cared." Then the quick drums, like a cat rattling pans in the kitchen, and Elvis is suddenly in her apartment, with candles all around ("Sun lights up the daytime, moon lights up the night").

Elvis embraces everything with a voice that runs the gauntlet from serial killer to altar boy ("Romeo and Juliet . . . Julie, baby, you're my flame, you give me fever"). The way Elvis sings "flame," he sounds like the devil. Then there's a single drum after "now give us fever" that thumps scarily and jumps around the stereo speakers.

As he sings "Captain Smith and Pocahontas had a very mad affair . . . when Daddy tried to kill him, she said 'Daddy don't you dare,'" the drums sound a tribal warning to protect an innocent lover. Elvis's "dare" is a righteous threat, sung with a woman's feathery vibrato. The bass line at the end is a canoe rowing slowly to the shore of an uncharted river. "What a lovely way to go."

Peggy serves Elvis a double Scotch on the rocks and puts her version of "Fever" on the turntable. Meanwhile, the King combs his hair in her mirror.

Little Willie John also recorded a delectable version of "Fever"; in fact, his rendition may be the best of all. Although Peggy Lee's performance of the song is sensual and titillating, Elvis's subtle yet lascivious heat—on the verge of zest—gives him the edge here.

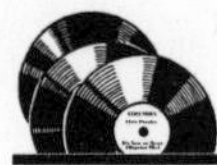

Such a Night

This song is not for the sexually inhibited. Elvis expresses deep arousal yet knows when to pull back. Others who sing with physical grit and fire—James Brown, Tom Jones, Tina Turner, Janis Joplin—are exciting in their own ways but sometimes come on too strong. Elvis, on the other hand, modulates emotions, exercising restraint when needed.

With Boots Randolph's tenor saxophone overriding the beginning of the song, "Such a Night" teases the listener with a different story. It's Brown's "I Can't Stand Myself (When You Touch Me)" on cruise control, Jones's "Delilah" but cooler, Turner's "Proud Mary" rollin' on the river without kicking up such a wake. Elvis, with a touch of humor in his voice, plays with the phenomenal boogie-woogie bass and piano roadhouse backbeat like a kitten toying with black stockings under the lovers' bed. Man, is this a racy song! "Such a kiss . . . just the thought of her lips" reveals Elvis in fellatio heaven—or something even more evolved. "Sweet surrender" never felt so good. The punctuated rhythm is reminiscent of Frank Sinatra's "Jealous Lover": "ba da da da bump" capturing the swing.

Yet there's more to come: "How well I remember, came the dawn and my heart and the night was gone . . . gone gone gone, came the dawn dawn dawn dawn . . . kiss kiss in the moonlight." Elvis is alone now but definitely not broken-hearted. He closes the song like a college frat boy bragging to his brothers ("Ooh ooh ooh—such a *night*"), the memory of the orgasmic encounter restrained, then bursting in his voice. The drummer goes almost psychotic, while Elvis lets out a "wooo," a paean to the mind-blowing experience of that night. Yeah, he scored big time.

However, there is also sincerity in Elvis's performance, blending with the macho posturing to create an indefinable romance full of playfulness, lust, and longing. Picture Brando in *The Wild One*, if he had the chance to spend the night with the waitress, all threat abandoned for now. Elvis hits an impressive balance. The Drifters' original of this song, although a fine record, is a pale moon obscured by Elvis's midnight sun.

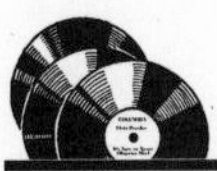

Like a Baby and **Reconsider Baby**

"Like a Baby" and "Reconsider Baby" are nothing like the blues that emerged in the Sun sessions. They're Chicago blues all the way—snarling and smoldering like the last jet in line for takeoff at O'Hare. On "Like a Baby," Elvis sings about all the misery he's been put through by his girl, but he's not on the mat, let alone down for the count. There's a bravado in his voice which proudly conveys that he has taken everything she can dish out, and he'll soon forget her anyway. Despite the bravado, "Like a Baby" is subdued somehow, a passenger easing into a window seat.

Joe Cocker once said, "Elvis Presley is the greatest blues singer in the world." Listen to "Reconsider Baby," particularly the way Elvis caresses the line "Oh, how I hate to see you go" like a Hollywood gigolo, not as a jilted, mournful lover. There's a threat in his voice, too, because he's daring the girl to find anyone who can satisfy her sexually the way he can. The sexuality and ominousness in the King's voice could detonate a studio—or Room 69 at the Beverly Hilton.

Elvis plays perhaps the best rhythm guitar of his career on "Reconsider Baby," achieving a smoldering sound, while Boots Randolph's sax work is as lethal as Mafia room service.

♦ ♦ ♦ ♦

In many ways, *Elvis Is Back* is a concept album—maybe the first—without ever intending to be. The opening two cuts are "Make Me Know It" and "Fever," followed by a very smooth cover of Ral Donner's "Girl of My Best Friend." Donner, who later narrated *This Is Elvis*, drew heavily from the King's style, so this was a bit of homage in reverse. "Make Me Know It" and "Fever" are full of feistiness and venom, while "Girl of My Best Friend" is hesitant, a young man staring through the department store window at the fancy bras and panty hose.

After "Soldier Boy" (the first cut on side two of *Elvis Is Back*—not the Shirelles' song), there are "Such a Night" and "It Feels so Right," songs brimming with hope, promise, and romance. Spliced between them and the final two blues numbers, the sultry "Like a Baby" and the wicked "Reconsider Baby," is "Girl Next Door Went a' Walking," a poignant song of pining and loss, the girl in her brand-new saddle shoes sashaying down the suburban avenue late at night, searching for "Paradise." Elvis stands at his open window, holding a microphone, all the spring leaves shaking slightly as he sings softly, so the couple walking down the street won't hear him.

The hints of "Teardrops" by the Hearts that we heard on "Soldier Boy," a reassuring song, are remembered now. *Elvis Is Back* is an elusive yet cohesive reflection on the mysteries of love. It may also be Elvis's most erotic album. It extends the possibilities of rock 'n' roll as a vehicle for exploring a central theme in multiple ways. Later, unmistakable concept albums include *Sergeant Pepper*, The Doors' self-titled first album, *Tommy* by the Who, and *The Joshua Tree* by U2.

While Elvis was filming his first movie since leaving the army, *G.I. Blues*, he was visited on set by the king and queen of Nepal, the king and queen of Thailand, the wife and daughter of the Brazilian

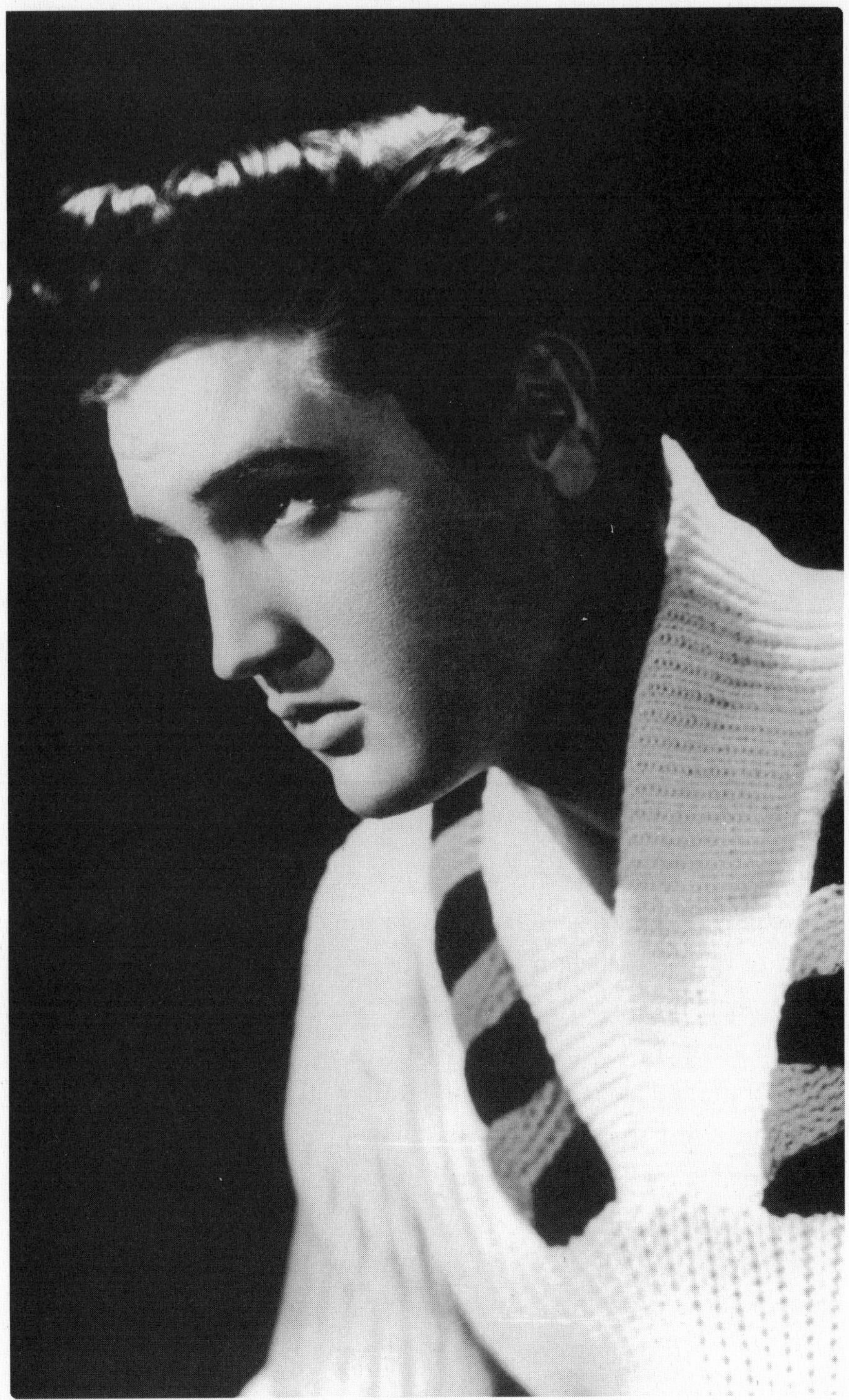

president, and princesses from Denmark, Norway, and Sweden. Each claimed to be a dedicated Presley devotee.

Elvis's co-star in *G.I. Blues* was Juliet Prowse, who was having an open affair with Frank Sinatra at the time. However, speaking candidly on national TV, Juliet related that she could not resist Elvis, who she thought was the sexiest of all men. Elvis and Juliet had a raucous and passionate affair that the public, and particularly Sinatra, didn't know about.

G.I. Blues was a smash at the box office. There were two reasons for this. First was the reinforcement of Elvis as the all-American boy. Second was the irony of the film's exploitation—for profit—of the political/military forces that had sought to exploit *him*. Elvis was caught in the middle. He had won but he had lost the edge to retaliate against the system.

♦ ♦ ♦ ♦

Now or Never *(Elvis: Worldwide 50 Gold Award Hits, Vol. 1, 1970)*

Recorded in 1960 during the *Elvis Is Back* sessions (as was "Are You Lonesome Tonight?" although neither song appeared on that album), "Now or Never" sold 10 million copies. Patterned after the light-classical Italian tune "O Sole Mio," this pop landmark almost portrays Elvis as an opera singer. Robert Matthew-Walker, English writer and classical music expert, notes that "Presley's first, stirring top E, strong and manly, sets the scene . . . the climax, with Presley soaring up to an incredible top G-sharp, is pure magic." Elvis handles the style as if he were born to it.

Elvis sang "Now or Never" many times in live performances, but none of those deliveries, including often slipshod phrasing, demonstrated the same intensity, flow, and precision that makes the studio version so urgent an ultimatum. He would hit the high notes in concert, but he sang so fast that he never quite captured the appeal and meaning of the original recording.

Are You Lonesome Tonight? *(Elvis: Worldwide 50 Gold Award Hits, Vol. 1, 1970)*

The 1960 studio release of "Lonesome Tonight" remains, next to "Love Me Tender," the premier example of Elvis's ability to exude calmness and confidence when expressing deep emotion at a human level to an audience. Billie Holiday and Frank Sinatra ("God Bless the Child," "It Was a Very Good Year," for instance) evoke similar intimacy and possibly more. Holiday and Sinatra were totally different artists, but the gift they shared is similar—the transference of peace to someone else—even if only for a few moments. These tastes of tranquillity sustain us through life's confusion.

Elvis's soliloquy at the center of the song ("Honey, you lied when you said you loved me") is like Hamlet's dagger. He follows with, "But I'd rather go on . . . ah . . . hearing your lies than to go on living without you." The pauses and the "ah" reveal inner turmoil, and when Elvis asks "Is you heart filled with pain, shall I come back again?" he shows that he truly cares more about her than himself. He's "standing there," right there, beside all of us, calm and collected, "with emptiness all around," as the supporting vocals "oooo" a lullaby.

Millie Kirkland's high-pitched backup vocals on the live 1969 version of "Lonesome Tonight" make that an equally memorable rendition.

♦ ♦ ♦ ♦

"Now or Never" and "Are You Lonesome Tonight?" were strong departures for Elvis, but they were two of his biggest-selling records.

The advantage that Elvis's manager, Colonel Tom Parker, saw in this was that resistant mainstream radio stations that had never played Elvis before now had both records on their turntables.

Joe Esposito records in his book *Good Rockin' Tonight* that during the filming of *Wild in the Country* (1961), Elvis had an affair with the notorious, enigmatic heartthrob Tuesday Weld, but the woman he was really interested in was his other co-star, Hope Lange. Elvis was maturing, but he still felt that Lange had too much class and sophistication for him, so he never approached her.

During the filming of the King's movies, he had amorous encounters with most of his leading ladies, as documented in *Elvis: What Happened*, the exposé by his former bodyguards.

♦ ♦ ♦ ♦

Can't Help Falling in Love (*Elvis: Worldwide 50 Gold Award Hits, Vol. 1*, 1970)

The piano opening is like a pendulum, a modulated "Ebb Tide" line, creating an almost hypnotic quality. Elvis gives a performance that disarms the listener with a combination of tenderness and insistence. Within the world of the song, there is no congestion, no confusion. Nothing can complicate the romantic purpose, despite the chaos and tragedy all listeners know too well. It is as though his feelings are immune to anything less than idealism and purity ("See how she leans her cheek upon her hand, O that I were a glove upon that hand, that I might touch that cheek").

Elvis's capacity for affection gives this performance its lasting magic. The song required several takes and some changes to make it what it is, but Elvis wasn't satisfied until he reached what Shakespeare promised was possible in *Romeo and Juliet*:

Give me my Romeo, and, when I die,
Take him and cut him out in little stars,
And he will make the face of heaven so fine
That all the world will be in love with night . . .

Although a different and unique record, John Lennon's "Imagine" evokes a purity similar to "Falling In Love."

"Can't Help Falling in Love" is from the musical *Blue Hawaii.* Before Elvis began the movie, however, he did a benefit concert to raise money for the USS *Arizona* memorial fund. When Elvis arrived in Honolulu, he was greeted by 2,500 screaming women at the airport. Jimmy Stewart was on the same plane, but when the actor got off, no one even recognized him. Fans pushed up against the fence, just trying to touch the King, as they shouted "Ellvviiss!"

The concert was held outdoors and turned into the longest performance that Elvis had given until that time. Yet the singing did not surge with the Banzai Beach rawness and power it had before his army years.

Rock-A-Hula Baby (*Blue Hawaii,* 1961)

Elvis seems to have fun with this piece of fluff from 1961's *Blue Hawaii*, and it suits the jovial, silly, Honolulu vacation-style choreography of the film. "Gotta hoola loo from a Honolu" is catchy stuff if you've had a couple of Primos at a fake luau. The sad part is that Elvis, in the early portion of a Hollywood career that spawned 31 films, already knew his movie career was going nowhere. His roles, as a boxer in *Kid Galahad* (1962) or a race car driver in *Spinout* (1966), are mostly predicable, sterile showcases of mediocrity.

At the end of "Rock-A-Hula Baby," Elvis becomes a parody of himself, belting out unconvincing blues cadences ("A well a rock, a hula baby, of miiiine") like a former champion of the world who has become a professional wrestler.

Of course, everybody has a good time and treks across the sand to the Royal Hawaiian for a nightcap.

The movie *Blue Hawaii* and the song "Rock-A-Hula Baby" are both embarrassing, but for most of the rest of the decade, things only got worse. The King also has the distinction of starring in some of the worst movies ever made. Elvis Presley dancing on the beach to "Slicin' Sand"? Even Mitch on *Baywatch* would have turned this one down! The fans should have protested against Colonel Parker and the big studios. In the end, however, Elvis allowed this to happen.

♦ ♦ ♦ ♦

Blue Hawaii was among Elvis's most financially successful movies, and it was one of the top-grossing films of 1961. This was probably the worst thing that could have happened to him. During this period, Elvis was doing a drama followed by a musical. Unfortunately, the Colonel was a formula man. Although the dramas made money, they didn't make as much profit as the musicals, particularly *Blue Hawaii*. After Parker saw the receipts from this film, there would be precious few dramas presented to Elvis.

Sources close to the King divulged that, although many diehard fans loved *Blue Hawaii*, Elvis did not. Publicly, he said he liked the film because he knew that was what his fans wanted him to say. Privately, however, he told friends it was a ridiculous movie. Angela Lansbury, who co-starred in the film, was also embarrassed by the project. There was one consolation for the King: he tumbled in the sand with his leading lady, Joan Blackman. There was also a gift to all of Elvis's female fans: "Can't Help Falling in Love."

♦ ♦ ♦ ♦

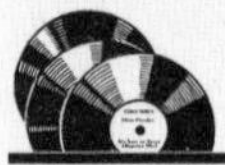

(Marie's the Name) His Latest Flame *(Elvis: The Other Sides; Worldwide Gold Award Hits, Vol. 2,* 1971)

A searing song, from the male point of view, about romance gone bad, without any hope whatsoever of reconciliation ("The prettiest green eyes anywhere, what else was there for me to do but cry?"). Yes, there are "Yesterday," "Tears of a Clown," and others, but the songs that most compare to the broken-hearted intensity of "His Latest Flame" are "Hurt" by Elvis Presley, "Backstreets" by Bruce Springsteen, "Earth Angel" by the Penguins and "Maybe" by the Chantels.

Elvis keeps his cool here, however, like a man is supposed to do; the Chantels could mourn openly. Yet his devastation oozes from every word and phrase, piercing the bravado ("Though I smile, the tears inside kept burnin'"). The rhythm guitar insistently repeats a simple chording pattern with little variation, and the piano pounds out repeated notes of loss in a high register during the refrains.

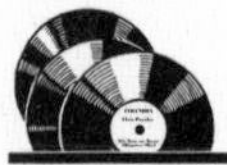

Little Sister *(Elvis: Worldwide 50 Gold Award Hits, Vol. 1,* 1970)

This was the original "A" side of the 45 that featured "His Latest Flame" on the "B" side. Both "Little Sister" and "Marie's the Name" are about lost love and abandonment. But while "Marie" is mournful and poetic, "Little Sister" becomes the true flip side of these feelings. The jilted lover here bites through the romance lingering in "Marie." The backup chorus on "Little Sister" ("Don't you do what your big sister done") sounds like a pack of Doberman pinschers, and Scotty Moore's ominous opening chords cast a dark spell over the song.

Keith Richards was undeniably influenced by Scotty in his intro to the Rolling Stones' fabulous "Last Time."

The lyric "Well, I used to pull your pigtails and pinch your turned up nose" makes "Little Sister" seem almost like a case of abuse. Once again, he's going to take big sister's rejection out on little sister ("Guess I'll try my luck with you"). Moore's guitar goes crazy.

"Don't you kiss me once or twice and say it's very nice—and then you *run*" reinforces this scenario. As does, especially, "You've been growin' and, baby, it's been showin' from your head down to your toes." Yet lurking in the background is another man ("We went for some candy, along came Jim Dandy, and they snuck right out the door"). Scotty's guitar is like a scream in the night.

All of Elvis's fury is targeted at two antagonists: big sister and Jim Dandy. The showdown with his adversary awaits—fireworks at noon. Meanwhile, the two sisters huddle on the porch swing, watching ("this may be the last time").

♦ ♦ ♦ ♦

The most provocative news on the Elvis front in 1962 involved his personal life. He had persuaded Priscilla Beaulieu's parents to let her live at Graceland. It seems irresponsible, at the very least, that they condoned this situation. Elvis also exhibited questionable judgment since, as Priscilla reveals in *Elvis and Me*, she was only 16 at the time. Elvis promised the Beaulieus that he would take care of Priscilla's schooling and everything else—and he guaranteed that the two lovers would sleep in separate rooms and would not have sex together until they married.

Some promises were kept; others were betrayed. The real point of this was that Elvis was raising Priscilla to be the perfect wife for him.

By her own account, Priscilla and Elvis did not have sexual intercourse but enjoyed passionate sex, although without penetration. As their sex life became more evolved, Priscilla would beg for him to come in her and consummate their love and passion for each other. Elvis portrayed diligent will power—he never relented—not just to satisfy her parents, but because he desperately wanted to marry a virgin.

Elvis was still putting out good singles, but his albums during this period were mostly musically weak soundtracks.

In 1963, Elvis was really beginning to hate the run of insipid movies he was starring in, and he was making noises about it. But he didn't really explode until a year later. In 1963, according to the polls and numbers, Elvis Presley was still the biggest star in the world.

Since there are different phases of Elvis's life, a brief look at how some friends described him around this time and later might prove revealing. Richard Davis, a member of the Memphis Mafia, said of Elvis, "You could live 10 lifetimes before you'll find another like him. He'll give you the shirt off his back. I love him."

Alan Fortas told this story: "My father was sick and dying, and I came to Memphis. Elvis said, 'You stay in Memphis, and if it's two years, you pick up your paycheck every week, and if you come back to work, you're fired. Go out to my house and pick up your check each week. Stay with your family.' And then he came to the hospital on Christmas and gave my father a gold pocket watch. He told me if there was anything I needed, don't hesitate."

There are many stories similar to this, but Elvis Presley also loved to have fun and revel in the company of good friends. *Elvis: What Happened* reveals that, although the King was not nearly as moody at this point as he would become in the 1970s, ill temper would sometimes jar the jocularity. Elvis was an enigmatic man, given to occasionally intense temper tantrums, as we shall see later in this book. It's interesting to note that the Memphis Mafia's nicknames for him ranged from "E" and "E1" to "Crazy."

Another demeaning film, *Fun in Acapulco*, was shot in 1963. Elvis's co-star, Ursula Andress, had a crush on him, despite the fact that she was dating John Derek, no slouch when it came to women. Andress's feelings for Elvis continued after the movie was made, and she called Graceland constantly. Eventually, Elvis stopped taking her calls—some say because Ursula was married to Derek. Over the years, Ms. Andress has proven to be a woman of class and substance.

Surrender (*Elvis: Worldwide 50 Gold Award Hits, Vol. 1,* 1970)

Elvis's inimitable voice and delivery make this the definitive version of "Surrender," which distills all the elements of an old silent movie into one quick song: melodrama laced with wit and passion. The tango/samba/rumba intro comes on like Desi Arnaz introducing the Sheik himself, Rudolph Valentino. The rhythm section pulsates like the *Mission Impossible* theme: Brazil to Cuba to Bedouin females in the background, Sahara winds swirling all around, kicking up their long robes, brushing sand from their eyes, revealing everything.

Elvis's voice insinuates itself softly at first ("When we kiss, my heart's on fire"), then more urgently ("burning with a strange desire"). A little later, when he sings, "so my darling, please surrender," the hissing sound on "so" is like a sidewinder slithering by the tent, but the delivery is also seductively delicate, hesitant, and charming. Elvis now becomes the Sheik and approaches her, singing "Let me hold you in my arms, dear, while the moon shines bright above," while the rhythm section enhances the song's weird darkness.

Elvis is as bold as an Arabian stallion when he declares, "All the stars will tell the story, of our love and all its glory," then briefly becomes a supplicant ("Surrender to me"), drawing out "me" gently and humorously, an oasis of desire. Then, "This night of magic . . . be mine tonight" explodes at the song's end. The background vocals fade into the storm like an old Victrola (shades of Gene Pitney's "Mecca"), and the Sheik disappears into the desert, chasing the ghost of Lawrence of Arabia.

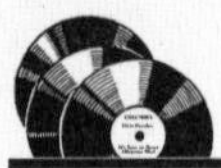

Return to Sender (*Elvis: Worldwide 50 Gold Award Hits, Vol. 1*, 1970)

A worthwhile pre-Beatles, early '60s pop rocker, "Return to Sender" did well on the charts during the "Please, Mr. Postman," "Mr. Lonely" period of American music. Elvis proves once again that he can blend seamlessly with a pop rock song without scarring a reputation spawned by revolution. There's just enough bite and grit in "Sender" to remind us of the '50s.

The line "If it comes back, the very next day, then I'll understand," evokes "My Baby Left Me," but there's not quite the same desperation in Elvis's voice here. Sure, he "sent it special D," but the earlier Elvis Presley would have kept knockin' till he couldn't come in.

Otis Blackwell wrote this fine composition for Elvis, while Boots Randolph's mournful saxophone evokes the image of a lonely tugboat returning to port after leading a cruise ship to the open sea.

It Hurts Me (*Elvis: The Other Sides; Worldwide Gold Award Hits, Vol. 2*, 1971)

This song was recorded in January 1964, the winter of the Beatles' and Stones' first appearances in America. Before Brian Epstein became their manager, the Beatles patterned themselves after Elvis. In the old photos from the German rock scene of the early '60s, the lads from Liverpool all look like Elvis—especially Stu Sutcliffe and John Lennon. John idolized the King and paid homage on more than a few occasions. He once declared, "Before Elvis, there was nothing." It seems fitting that, when Elvis was among the 10 artists initially enshrined in the Rock 'n' Roll Hall of Fame in 1986, John's son Julian handled the induction honors.

"It Hurts Me" begins with a moody "Sea of Love"-style piano, like counting shells on the shore while dejectedly watching the sun go down in quick colors of gold, orange, silver. Elvis sings slowly, hesitantly ("It hurts me to see him treat you the way that he does"), as if he were walking alone on the beach. When the sense of injustice is delicately revealed ("The whole town is talking . . . calling you a fool for listening to his same old lies"), Elvis is almost in need of CPR. Yet the spirit of righteousness moves him to gather strength ("It hurts me to see the way he makes you cry-y-y"), and he draws out the word "cry" in anguish as the piano crashes like surf on the rocks. Then, his delivery becomes soft as the salty breeze ("You love him so much, you're too blind to see") and the whole song moves up and down like sets of waves rolling toward shore. The ending is a crescendo of caring—passionate yet perfectly controlled ("Waiting to hold you so tight, waiting . . . yes darlin', to find someone like you").

"It Hurts Me" is a mourning song, and Elvis's performance brings to mind Timi Yuro's "Hurt" (covered by Elvis, reviewed in this book), Little Anthony's "Hurts So Bad," Toni Fisher's "The Big Hurt" ("Now it begins, needles and pins, twilight to dawn"), and the Spinners' "I'll Be Around" ("a tiny spark that remains, and sparks turn into flames"). These songs are all about rejection and pain—and hope. Yet when Elvis sings, "I know that he never will set you free, 'cause he's just that kinda guy," there is a gentle cosmic acceptance of the way things stand—of fate—and even a touch of humor. Timi Yuro's fake crying and the Spinners' "there's always a chance" capture this saving grace also.

♦ ♦ ♦ ♦

Elvis's best musical, *Viva Las Vegas* (*Jailhouse Rock* and *King Creole* are more dramas than musicals), was filmed in 1963 and co-starred Ann-Margret, one of the world's sexiest and most passionate women.

She has since become one of the finest and classiest actresses, and remains a big fan of Elvis Presley. Interestingly, she came to the United States from her native Sweden billed as the "female Elvis."

As she reminisced during a TV interview, sparks immediately flew between Ann-Margret and Elvis, and the two carried on a torrid love affair during the filming of *Viva Las Vegas*. Ann-Margret said recently that "the tremendous passion between us couldn't be resisted." Their affair grew into a genuine relationship. This was the first and only time in Elvis's life that he actually considered sending Priscilla back to her parents and marrying someone else. When Ann-Margret Smith's autobiography was released a few years ago, she confessed on television that Elvis was indeed the love of her life.

Elvis's bodyguards and other members of the Memphis Mafia confirm that Priscilla was very jealous of her rival and even tried to copy Ann-Margret's style of dress, hair, and behavior in an effort to keep Elvis for herself. This testifies to Priscilla's insecurity at the time, as well as Elvis's cavalier treatment of their relationship.

♦ ♦ ♦ ♦

(You're the) Devil in Disguise *(Elvis: Worldwide 50 Gold Award Hits, Vol. 1, 1970)*

The early 1960s saw American popular music move into its first truly "pop" period. By this we mean that rock 'n' roll, as well as r&b, was beginning to respond to the lure of formula. Yes, there had always been categories of music—delta blues, Chicago blues, rockabilly, etc.—but now, a new trend was being established, one that (contrary to doo-wop of the '50s, for example) relied on quick fixes to satisfy the emerging teens of the baby-boom generation, who were also becoming a significant source of record sales.

This is not to say that great music wasn't made during this period. Elvis produced several outstanding records, as did Ray Charles. And just listen to Gary "U.S." Bonds' "Quarter to Three," Phil Spector's awesome production of the Crystals' "And Then He Kissed Me," and many others. However, there was much more calculation than spontaneity to the music of the early '60s. Spector was the master; "Da Do Ron Ron," "Be My Baby," and "He's a Rebel" are masterpieces of ingenuity and doctoring a groove. The Beach Boys followed suit, and Motown was kicking into gear toward the end of this era, around 1963.

Enter Elvis with "Devil in Disguise." The early '60s were a strange period in his career. His first album after completing his military service in 1960 was *Elvis Is Back,* which is full of introspection and vitality.

Listen to the beginning of Bobby Vee's number-one hit "Take Good Care of My Baby" and you'll hear the intro to "Devil in Disguise," which is slightly speeded up. The start of Dick and Deedee's "The Mountains High" (number one for several weeks in 1962) has the same feel.

"Devil in Disguise" is a "Runaround Sue" kind of song, maybe even Del Shannon's great "Runaway" ("You fooled me with your kisses, you cheated and you schemed; heaven knows how you lied to me—you're not the way you seem"). There's a delicate autoharp in the rhythm section, recalling how this instrument was used in so many '50s songs, among them "Pretty Blue Eyes" by Steve Lawrence and "Dream Lover" by Bobby Darin. Listen closely and you can even hear Jimmy Gilmer and the Fireballs' "Sugar Shack" (number one in '63), with its superpop melding of country, blues, and rock.

Although Elvis sings tough and accusatory here ("I thought that I was in heaven, but I was sure surprised, heaven help me, I didn't see the devil in your eyes"), "Devil in Disguise" is really streamlined, lightweight radio fare that lacks the menacing edge of "Little Sister" or the reverie of "Marie's the Name." The hand clapping and the low bass voice at the end ("oh yes you are)" tease the listener into an expectation of danger, but it's really only the parody of a threat. Elvis is toying with the pop genre here, and "Devil in Disguise" is as fine an example of that easy, digestible innocence as Bobby Vee's "Devil or Angel" or the Chiffons' "He's So Fine."

"Devil in Disguise" can't touch the best of Phil Spector or early Motown, but it clearly demonstrates the ease with which Elvis could slip into a new genre. Or, maybe it was a progression—his music had been heading in that direction, perhaps because Elvis hated his movies and had begun losing his interest in performing. The chance to mix it up with the new kids on the block revitalized the King's reputation as the one who started it all, the one still lurking in the shadows, ready for anything.

♦ ♦ ♦ ♦

In 1964, Elvis made his strongest stand against the numbing movies, which he called "travelogues." His bodyguards recount that Presley went to Colonel Parker determined to not make any more of these ridiculous travesties which, he said, made him "physically sick." The Colonel didn't want to change the formula of the movies because they were still making money. Additionally, he said there was nothing to remedy the dilemma because he and Elvis were bound by "the Hollywood contracts."

Elvis was in awe of Hollywood, which saw the King as its golden calf, and felt that the town could destroy him. He thought about challenging the Hollywood studios—and the Colonel—on his own, but he ultimately did not have the courage to do so. According to Steve Binder, the noted television music show producer who directed and produced *Elvis*, later known as *The '68 Comeback Special*, "The fact that Elvis's name could make any picture profitable was more of a reason to make good movies."

This was one of the situations that made Colonel Tom Parker

an albatross for Elvis. Parker did well by his client in the 1950s, but forcing the King to do these inane films was an insult. There is no denying that Elvis's movies helped to make him more famous throughout the world; however, they took a great toll on his artistic reputation. Perhaps fans who made the movies so popular are also responsible.

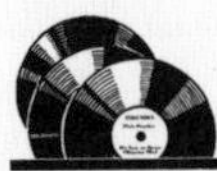

Memphis *(Elvis for Everyone, 1965)*

It is beyond belief that Elvis Presley could render such an uninspired, even lackadaisical performance of the signature song of his adopted hometown. Graceland's blinds and curtains cover all the windows when this one comes on the radio; the servants and chauffeurs pretend they don't work there; and streams of fans look at one another in shock, asking, "Is that really Elvis?"

Unfortunately, the answer is yes. There are no vocal inflections or intonations whatsoever to cook this backwoods squirrel stew. The reading of this Chuck Berry song is flat and monotonous, never achieving Berry's flair or sense of hopelessness. There is no break in Elvis's pitch, and the awkward rhythm section overpowers his weakly mixed voice, playing too fast, as if they can't wait to end the session.

The guitar break sounds like a kid playing his first solo at the high school prom; you can barely hear it. Johnny Rivers did a fair take on "Memphis," capturing the song's weird, sultry quality.

Sorry. Elvis's date dances with another guy this time around.

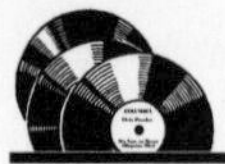

For the Millionth and Last Time (*Elvis For Everyone,* 1965)

With a pseudo-Latin/tango-style beat that sounds like a mutant cross between "How Much Is That Doggie in the Window" and "Never on Sunday," "For the Millionth and Last Time" almost makes "Old Shep," Elvis's worst song, look like a purebred. Please, put on "Old Rivers," Walter Brennan's soppy ode to his mule—anything but this! At least "Doggie" and "Sunday" were cute songs, one for children, the other for hookers with hearts of gold. ("Shep" and "Rivers" can still be seen playing cards in velveteen paintings above a million fireplaces.)

The title is excessive, the lyrics insoluble, and Elvis delivers such gems as "a million or so kisses ago we said goodnight at your door" weakly, with no energy. Well, that's understandable—a *million* kisses? No wonder he's tired. The thing is, they never made it ("I didn't get far, 'cause here we are, and I'm still begging for more"). Unbelievable! The King needs an ice-cold shower after getting knocked out of the box by this girl—or that hooker with a heart of diamond.

By 1966, Elvis wasn't feeling good about himself or his career. Although it seemed as though he were merely stagnating, he was really going downhill. The soundtrack albums and the movies had become, if possible, even worse.

Friends close to Elvis believe his personal life mirrored the downward spiral of his career. He still didn't know whether to marry Priscilla, and everything in his life was a tired, exasperating routine. Elvis became difficult to live with, as his temper and foul moods were much more in evidence. Most regrettably, his consumption of prescription drugs was increasing. Surely, his intake of drugs was nowhere near what it would be in the 1970s, but it had increased markedly since the early '60s.

The major sign that Elvis was bored and depressed about his career and personal life was that he would often withdraw behind the gates of Graceland. Yet he was much too young and vital to star in his own production of *Sunset Boulevard.* He would rewrite that script later.

The first hints of revival occurred when Elvis chose meaty songs to supplement the movie numbers. For example, when there wasn't enough material to complete the *Spinout* soundtrack, Elvis selected three excellent songs to cut in the studio and include on the album. The most notable of these tunes is Bob Dylan's brilliant "Tomorrow Is a Long Time."

♦ ♦ ♦ ♦

Tomorrow Is a Long Time (*Spinout,* 1966)

At first, Elvis didn't like Bob Dylan—he was turned off by the folksinger's odd-sounding voice. But he gradually came to admire Dylan's beautiful poetry, and when Elvis heard "Tomorrow Is a Long Time," he became a fan and felt he simply had to record the song himself.

Dylan once said, "Elvis recorded a song of mine. That's the one recording I treasure most." This is the song, and that reverence is reciprocated, from Elvis's opening "mmmm" (accompanied by tambourine and finger-lickin' country guitar pickin') to the final "oooh, mmmm," repeated three times, like a prayer. Elvis's performance here is different from anything he had done previously; it's revealing and special in its sense of understatement. The King sounds so shell-shocked that his usual personality is unrecognizable, as if he can't remember his "own name."

"Tomorrow" was recorded in 1966, at the height of Dylan's influence on song lyrics via *Highway 61* (1965) and *Blonde on Blonde* (1966). Elvis's internal harmony caresses the words like a preacher baptising him on a Sunday morning ("There's beauty in the silver, singin' river, there's beauty in the sunrise in the sky").

This is a cleansing, resurrecting song, yet it is also filled with grief ("If only she was lying by me, then I'd lie in my bed once again"). No, this isn't "Lay Lady Lay," a later Dylan song (*Nashville Skyline*, 1969) with an easy, sexy, country feel—and Elvis intuits the difference expertly. "I can't speak the sounds that show no pain" echoes across the tombstones as Elvis hears "her heart softly pounding," and awaits tomorrow.

Elvis Presley loved gospel music, and anyone who doubts the King's deep religious commitment should listen to the full catalog. For example, the RCA albums *His Hand in Mine* (1960), *How Great Thou Art* (1967), and *He Touched Me* (1972) all received five stars in *The Rolling Stone Album Guide*.

The five songs that follow are indicative of Elvis's reverence and religious fervor.

♦ ♦ ♦ ♦

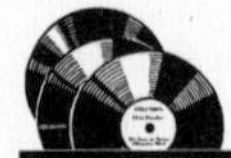

Crying in the Chapel (*How Great Thou Art*, 1967)

Originally recorded in October 1960, "Chapel" was not released until April 1965 as a single, and it soared to number three on the *Billboard* chart in the middle of Beatlemania and the British Invasion. Perhaps the rise of the Civil Rights movement with Dr. Martin Luther King, the escalation of the war in Vietnam, and the budding of the counterculture in the heart of the Great Society had something to do with this song touching our hearts—and creating a place of refuge and hope amid increasing confusion about who we were and where we were going.

"Crying in the Chapel" was Elvis's last gold single until 1968's "If I Can Dream," a protest song. That would be followed by a socially conscious movie, *Change of Habit*, and then by Elvis's stirring protest number "In the Ghetto." These songs demonstrate Elvis's sensitivity to the tumultuous times of the '60s, with the accent on reconciliation, rather than confrontation. These candles easing the chaos were lighted by Elvis Presley—a son of the Old South.

There is no instrumental introduction here; Elvis rushes straight into "Chapel" like Rafael with a fresco. "The tears I shed were tears of joy" is sung in a voice rich as Chianti, while the Jordanaires' "oooooooo" chorus is smooth as virgin olive oil. "Now I'm happy in the chapel, where people are of one accord," is so beautifully delivered that we can almost see the newlyweds as they emerge, hand in hand, enveloped in sunlight, on the way to the feast. Elvis sings calmly and assuredly, "Take your troubles to the chapel, get down on your knees and pray," the words not a command but a faithful plea.

Peace in the Valley *(A Legendary Performer, Vol. 2, 1974)*

President Dwight David Eisenhower said he would support Hungary if it were invaded by the Soviet Union, but when the Soviets moved in to crush an anti-Communist uprising, the United States backed down. This resulted in much devastation in Hungary, and caused more than 190,000 people to become refugees. When Elvis first performed this song, on his third appearance on *The Ed Sullivan Show*,

January 6, 1957, he dedicated "Peace" to those refugees and to other victims of the Soviet massacre.

Elvis sings as if this song were a traditional spiritual, resulting in a sound that is more black than white. His vocals demonstrate his absorption of black culture, desegregated, melding so beautifully with his white gospel roots that the two become virtually indistinguishable.

A stirring, steadfast gospel favorite, "Peace in the Valley" is an affirmation ("the lion shall lay down by the lamb") that all fears in "the night . . . black as the sea" will soon be allayed, brightened by the sun. Elvis humbly makes a plea for peace in his own way ("Oh, Lord, I pray"), returning to the roots that nourished him. At the close of *The '68 Comeback Special*, Elvis would sing a new song, "If I Can Dream," in memory of Dr. King and Senator Robert F. Kennedy, more vigorously—even desperately.

"Peace in the Valley" eerily anticipates "Dream"; the lyrics and music are quite similar, yet they are rendered differently. One might have been sung in a church that had received a bomb threat on Sunday, the other in the church where the bomb had already exploded.

"Peace" is performed so movingly by Elvis and the male chorus—their "oooo's" blending with his "oh oh oh, yes" like a candle flame against stained-glass windows—that the people in the congregation cannot help but feel "changed, changed from the creature" they have become.

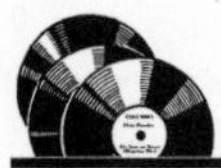

You'll Never Walk Alone (*How Great Thou Art*, 1967)

This sweet song was written by Rodgers and Hammerstein. "Walk Alone" has been sung for decades by Baptist choirs, Catholic school kids, Jewish vocal ensembles, a couple trudging along a bleak highway toward distant lights after a breakdown, their voices rising above the frightful sounds of night. Some songs just have that kind of impact; they bring out the best in whoever is singing them. Elvis becomes the Archangel Gabriel, perhaps Abraham himself, channeling all of these voices into his own heart, sure of his power to communicate the pain, passion, and longing of our human condition. This may be the one to play after your lover has gone, and faith is a memory.

Elvis's voice hits every note, every nuance of meaning, like Elmer Gantry in a steamy Bible Belt revival tent, the congregation rapturous, surging toward the stage, pledging everything. Sure, you can contribute. What have you got to give—belief in yourself and other people. That's where Elvis differs from Gantry.

Elvis sings "Walk on through the wind," as though "on" were the siren of a rescue vehicle speeding toward a desolate rest stop. The piano, spare at first, builds into a storm, then pounds as fervently as Hail Marys prayed in a cellar as the twister gets closer and closer. Elvis stretches "You'll ne-eee-ver walk a-ah-lo-oh-hone" into a cry of assurance. The soft background harmony of male voices serves as understated counterpoint to Elvis's dedication. The piano is the sole musical support, and the whole performance is reminiscent of the aching "Unchained Melody" (live, 1977).

How Great Thou Art (*How Great Thou Art,* 1967)

If Elvis had recorded only this song, and someone found a disty tape in an abandonded Georgia church, his genius would still have been recognized. That's how strong "How Great Thou Art" is. The album of the same name didn't sell in the millions, nor did his other gospel recordings: *His Hand in Mine, He Touched Me,* etc. These albums were made not for the money but because Elvis believed in them. Those who charge that Elvis became commercial and sold out don't take into account the gospel LPs.

Similarly, when Elvis played Las Vegas in 1969, he didn't care if he made a dime—he was determined to put on the greatest concerts of his career. Besides the rock 'n' roll band, the King wanted a big 30-piece orchestra on stage to accentuate a particular movement or karate ending, to add electricity. Also, the "Priscilla ballads," songs that reflected his pain over losing his wife, weren't recorded to make money but to express Elvis's feelings. The many "Priscilla ballads" and the albums that included them did not do well commercially.

"How Great Thou Art" and the other gospel performances tell different stories. It's a shame that more people—even to this day—still don't know that Elvis did this splendid work. On "How Great Thou Art," he sheds all of the popular perceptions of his persona—steeped in gospel, country, and blues, but ultimately rebellious, rejecting the core of his roots to forge an anarchistic rock 'n' roll identity. Well, that's true, yet nothing could be further from reality. Elvis remains mysterious.

When he sings, "Oh Lord, my God," after the "ah ah ah ah" of the black female chorus, it's as if "in awesome wonder" he has been born again. The piano undulates like windblown fields of grain on "I see the stars," while drums rumble after "I hear the rolling thunder." Then, the exquisitely enunciated "the universe displayed," breathes softly as the Milky Way. The chorus buoys this transcendence impeccably. "Joy shall fill my heart" is a Confirmation procession of sound. Yet it's the conclusion that lingers. The last "How great Thou art" rings as resoundingly as the last words of Revelation: "The grace of the Lord Jesus be with you all. Amen!" The chorus's final note pierces like cathedral bells at dawn.

He Is My Everything (*He Touched Me*, 1972)

Elvis receives full accompaniment on "Everything" but is never overshadowed by his cohorts, who supplement his sincerity. The strings enter gently and discreetly, like a child approaching the altar for his first Communion, while Elvis prays "I want to bow down before Him, and hear Him say 'well done.' " The line "the reason for living, oh He is the King of all Kings" stands out, a dedication of life and vocation to the highest power.

"He Is My Everything" contains country/gospel and jazz elements, from the opening guitar—a combination of folk mass freshness and Larry Coryell fusion—to the perfectly syncopated female chorus, guitar, drums, and cymbals that enhance "I long to be His possession." Elvis shows us all the way like a wayward son returning home for a family reunion, smiling once again at all the faces he has ever really cared about.

This gospel ballad features the same music as the country ballad "There Goes My Everything." Elvis recorded both songs but is clearly more committed to the gospel version, engendering more conviction. As a result, his majestic baritone sounds much richer on the religious song. "He Is My Everything" bears testimony to the deep humility that Elvis always possessed, even in troubled times, maybe especially then.

♦ ♦ ♦ ♦

In 1965, Elvis made a movie called *Tickle Me*, which co-starred Julie Adams and Jocelyn Lane. Newscasts in this pre-*Hard Copy* period pricked up their ears because Ms. Lane was a real princess, born of royal blood. According to the Memphis Mafia, the last thing she wanted to do was meet this crazy guitar slinger, let alone make a picture with him.

But this was not the same Elvis who had shied away from Hope Lange several years before. This Elvis was now confident that he could be in the presence of a woman of higher social standing and still impress her. The King and the princess had a sovereign fling. The two tickled themselves in all the right places and ended up dating during the shooting of the film. The tabloids picked up on the affair, but if the same thing happened today, the supermarket sheets would be almost too hot to touch.

U.S. Male *(Double Dynamite, Pickway, 1976)*

The 1967 single is a clever, funny spoof of country/western machismo packaged with some tantalizing pickin', strummin', and percussion, especially after the two "you better not mess with a U.S. Male" choruses, when the musicians flirt with funky jazz-rock time signatures. The introductory spoken personal history parodies Elvis's fondness for story-like segues within songs. "Now, Mississippi just happens to occupy a place in the southeastern portion of this here United States," is delivered with mock "country bumpkin" humor, as if he's responding to a hopelessly lost driver from Boston, at a gas station in Tupelo, who has asked where Mississippi is.

Imagine Elvis singing the story break to "Are You Lonesome Tonight?" this way: "Now the stage is bare, and you're standing there, without any hair." That's the kind of tone he toys with on "U.S. Male." It reminds one of "Hot Rod Lincoln" or "Boy Named Sue," but cuts with a sharper edge, is more satirical.

Elvis drawls like a good ol' boy at the bar of Joe Ray Bob's saloon: "I catch you 'round my woman, champ, I'm gonna leave your head like the shape of a stamp." Don't forget, Elvis is "a U.S. M-A-L-E, son, that's me"—he spells it out at one point and is proud of it. But he's really the Postmaster General, M-A-I-L, and feels compelled to elaborate to Don Juan ("kinda flattened out") as if he's fought this fight before. Elvis is also portraying Uncle Sam—in the middle of the Vietnam War, with a serious tilt to his voice—and at the same time lampooning the character he has created.

Listen closely to the fadeout at the end, where the rough line "You're talkin' to the *American* U.S. Male" is a slight imitation of Lyndon Baines Johnson. This is as close as Elvis ever gets to being Lenny Bruce; he becomes the President of rock 'n' roll.

Big Boss Man *(Clambake,* 1967)

Nineteen sixty-seven was the year of "Light My Fire," "White Rabbit," "Purple Haze," the Summer of Love, counterculture. "Big Boss Man" fit into the hip scene like an 18-wheeler pulling up at the commune in Marin County. It's an anachronism—God forbid, it's uncool! *Clambake?* What's a clambake, man? Fifties stuff, oh yeah, groovy. A few years after Elvis sang, "Gonna get me a new boss man, one that'll treat me right," the Who spat out "Meet the new boss, same as the old boss." Yeah, baby, "tune in, turn on, drop out."

Elvis had no taste for this, but with his recordings of "U.S. Male," "Big Boss Man," "Guitar Man," and "Hi-Heel Sneakers," he foreshadowed the complex spirit of *The '68 Comeback Special.*

So let's just end this essay right now and chalk "Big Boss Man" up to nostalgia. Not quite. This song is as tightly structured as the lunchtime whistle at a steel mill. The harmonica throughout plays red hot bars that are cooled by the jazzy, Stax-influenced horns. Elvis's vocals are delightful, half-serious ("Can't you hear me when I call?") and half-humorous ("You're just tall, that's all"), quite similar to what Dylan was doing around the same time with "Rainy Day Women" and the Beatles were exploring with *Sergeant Pepper.*

Out of date? Not really. Elvis stuck to his truck-drivin' roots and sang a protest song that the younger generation could *not* relate to at the time. They can all relate to it now. "Got to serve somebody" (Dylan).

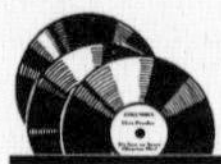

Hi-Heel Sneakers *(Elvis Aron Presley, 1980)*

The silent comeback of 1967 is well represented by this sleazy, sexy, blues-funk ditty. Elvis slips into the cocky vocal like a pimp donning a pair of snakeskin boots, ready for some action ("Well, I'm pretty sure now, baby, pretty soon you're gonna knock 'em dead"). Somebody in the band groans "oohm" right after "baby," an orgasm in the back seat of a Chevy Caprice at the end of Twelfth Street. There will be no resistance, or she will have to pay a price.

"Slap that wig right on your head" is sung with venom; it's as cold as Dirty Harry's "Do you feel lucky?" but with a jaunty beat, a mock playfulness that makes it even more chilling. The twangy yet slithery guitar sets a decadent mood—almost a sitar sound—as it blends with brooding drums and hand claps, and especially Charlie McCoy's repetitive, cobra-charming harmonica line. Elvis's "na na na na na na na I I I I I I . . ." scat funk is as hypnotic as a tribal chief's war chant. This is the kind of performance that would make the shyest lady in the club get up and dance on the table, twirling her sweater over her head. "All right, take it home, baby," Elvis drawls. The night is young!

Elvis and Priscilla married in 1967, and the ceremony and the pictures from it occupy a cherished place in the annals of celebrity weddings. Priscilla (Elvis referred to her as "Cilla") declares in her book *Elvis and Me* that on the night of the wedding, she and the King finally consummated their love for each other. She adds that, for the next few months, the couple experienced fabulous, passionate sex.

But when Priscilla became pregnant, the great lovemaking ended. Elvis had a "mother conflict"; having never really recovered from Gladys' death, he considered sex with any mother figure to be almost sacrilegious. Although he tried, he found the task very distasteful. Over the next five years, the King and his queen had sex only about 50 times, Priscilla laments in her book. During those encounters, Elvis never exhibited the passion he had displayed earlier. After the birth of their baby, however, Elvis found solace on the side, while Priscilla languished and yearned at home, growing more and more frustrated. For a brief period, she had the first of two affairs, but Priscilla felt very guilty and soon broke off the relationship.

CHAPTER 4

Burbank: Transcending the Legend

With a wife and baby, Elvis felt good about his personal life. And he was recording better material, such as "Guitar Man" and "Hi-Heel Sneakers," but the songs didn't do well commercially. By 1968, Elvis's career had ebbed because of inferior soundtracks and inane movies. He hadn't had a gold record in three years, and his films were barely in the black. As a result, Elvis and his manager, Colonel Tom Parker, agreed to do a television special with producer/director Steve Binder. As Jerry Hopkins, author of *Elvis*, stated, Binder had gained his reputation from producing the acclaimed rock special *T.A.M.I.*, during which James Brown actually intimidated Mick Jagger with his outrageous movements. However, once the Stones, who also appeared on the special, got their balance, they kicked out the jams.

Binder and the Colonel had different ideas about what the show's format should be. Parker wanted a Christmas special, while Binder wanted a rock 'n' roll program. Elvis sided with Binder; Parker tasted a nasty defeat.

The show was entitled *Elvis* and later became known as *The '68*

Comeback Special and also as the "Burbank sessions." The sit-down shows, in which the King and his fellow musicians sat in a semicircle on a small, slightly elevated stage, surrounded by the audience, were performed at 6:00 P.M. and 8:00 P.M. on June 29, 1968. The stand-up shows, in which Elvis sang and danced on a makeshift, boxing-ring-style stage set up in the middle of the crowd, took place at 6:00 P.M. and 8:00 P.M. on June 29.

From these shows, RCA compiled a single-disc LP entitled *Elvis*, which was released in December 1968, the same month the special aired on NBC. Both the TV special and the RCA album featured selected performances from the sit-down and stand-up shows; the special also showcased a few production numbers, such as "Little Egypt" and "Big Boss Man."

After the King's death, two double-disc bootleg albums were released: *The Burbank Sessions, Vol. 1*, containing material from the sit-down shows, and *The Burbank Sessions, Vol. 2*, featuring selections from the stand-up shows. However, RCA's *Elvis* remains the only legitimate recording of the Burbank sessions.

Lawdy, Miss Clawdy (*Elvis* [RCA], 1968; *The Burbank Sessions, Vol. 1*)

Elvis first recorded this song in the 1950s, turning it into a good rocker. If you compare the '50s version with *The Burbank Sessions'* rendition, however, the original sounds amateurish, incapable of capturing the potential of the song. In 1968, Elvis performs as though possessed; he's so hot he could melt steel. The effect sizzles enough to make the neighbors call the vice squad.

Elvis begins by uttering "Well, well, well . . . ," rolls his head a few times, then rips into this brief blues tale about leaving a woman who has done him wrong. He comes to grips with being "down in misery" in bold fashion, grimacing, sneering, even striking the pose of a bullfighter making a pass after the line "Please don't excite me, baby." He spits out the vow "gonna tell, tell my mama, I swear to God, what you been doin' " like a lover on the verge of hiring a hit man, or perhaps Polk Salad Annie's "razor totin' mama"! Elvis can't resist a little laugh after "You like to ball every morning"—half mischievous, half embarrassed, which makes it sting even harder. When he finishes with "don't come home 'til late that night," one of the band members cries, "Oh yeah." Female screams fill the room.

The song ends with Elvis's voice hammering Miss Clawdy's coffin closed forever ("down the road I go—da da da da da da da da da da—da da da"). For now, there are no tears.

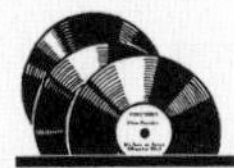

Baby, What You Want Me to Do (*The Burbank Sessions, Vol. I*)

This song is a boogie stampede of Elvis's resplendent lead guitar, volatile vocals, and inspired backup work by Scotty Moore and D. J. Fontana. Elvis varies the speed of his picking and strumming like a cattle-drive ramrod controlling the herd in a cloud of dust: gentle yet puncturing notes one moment, then rhythmic chords as savage as a raider's arrows. "Ride 'em in, let 'em out, cut 'em out, ride 'em in, let 'em out, cut 'em out, ride 'em in, *Rawhide*"—it's shades of Frankie Laine but not quite so fast.

The strange thing is, "Baby, What You Want Me to Do" is about having sex, and the frustration involved in finding it. Elvis's sinuous, dirty blues vocals tell the story ("We're goin' up, we're goin' down, we're goin' up down, down up, any way you wanna be rolled . . . yeah yeah yeah"), sung hard as horses' hooves. The King's opening words are "Oh get dirty, baby." The instrumental break (not quite an Elvis guitar solo but breathtaking work nonetheless) is like a freight train approaching from a great distance, rumbling slowly at first, then thundering down the rails. The band members shout to one another ("All right"—"uh uh, all right"—"Oh yeah, get it") while Elvis plays furiously and concludes the break with "Hep hep hep . . ." then, leaning back, "Mmmm!" Fontana thumps on his drum case like a warrior—he did not set up his drum kit for the session.

Elvis finishes the song almost as if he were in a dream ("You got me peepin', you got me hidin', you got me peep hide, hide anyway you wanna roll"). Elvis ain't gonna hide no more. He's ready for anything or anybody. "True love . . . waiting at the end of my ride."

Trying to Get to You *(The Burbank Sessions, Vol. 1; A Legendary Performer, Vol. 1, 1974)*

Elvis begins "Tryin' to Get to You" with steady, confident determination as he sings "I've been travelin' over mountains, even through the valleys too. I've been travelin' night and day . . . runnin' all the way, baby, tryin' to get to you." This song hits on the "boy wants girl back" motif, but he's going to have to go get her. Here, he already has—the song is written in the past tense ("There were many miles between us, but they didn't mean a thing"). Yet, like most of the material on the 1968 sit-down shows, there's a lot more going on.

Elvis belts out "There was nothin' that could hold me, or could keep me away from you," in fervent blues/rock, even soul style. His performance is not just intense and ferocious, it's a revival. Elvis is not just here to duplicate the past but to completely reinvent himself. He bursts through the song as if trying to get to the essence of himself, as well as the woman of his dreams. His arresting voice and guitar playing electrify the room, and by song's end, he's overcome, his

head shaking back and forth, almost in a trance. Finally, Elvis raises his right hand in victory like a gold-medal winner holding high the Olympic torch.

Tiger Man (*The Burbank Sessions, Vol. 1; Elvis Singing "Flaming Star" and Others,* 1968)

The old Rufus Thomas tune is supercharged by Elvis at the 8:00 P.M. sit-down show. Having taken over electric lead guitar duties earlier on the fine "Blue Christmas" (moving Scotty Moore to acoustic rhythm), Elvis plays here with the frenzied precision of an ax murderer. The repetitive, rhythmic lead pattern stings like high-voltage barbed wire, and Elvis's body twitches as he growls "If you cross my path, you take your own life in your hands." During the "DA da da da da da . . ." scat vocal breaks, Elvis harmonizes with the warp-speed strumming, a ravenous predator gnawing its prey. D. J. Fontana beats out time on a guitar case as if he fears for his life, while Moore seems stunned or hypnotized, his rhythm chords barely audible.

Elvis sways and moves almost as if seeking to avoid the myth of his past ("The hound dogs stay way back, way back, way back," "Lions play too rough"), while the girls in the audience scream wildly, evoking memories of the early days. Through all of the intensity, there's a twinkle in Elvis's eyes. He seems ready to stop the song and drawl, "Only kiddin', man." The shadow of his smile reminds everyone, "Tigers ain't the kind you'd rather love." That was *always* Elvis's greatest charm : his fusion of passion and fun.

At the end of "Tiger Man," Elvis winds down ("Ain't no end to this song, baby"), and after a few seconds, one of his sidemen yells, "You got it." Yes he does. Then, Elvis does a parody of "MacArthur Park" that is worthy of Robin Williams, singing "I don't think that I can make it, cause it took so long to bake it" in an extremely high register, mocking Richard Harris's angst. The tiger is suddenly playing with the audience—and they love it. Elvis has found a new "recipe," and he's really cookin'!

In the 1950s, pop idol Fabian released a song called "Like a Tiger" that contained the immortal line "I wanna growl—wow," sung playfully. Fabian was one of many Elvis imitators—cute, Elvis haircut, nice guy, helped his family, a good kid—and, like teen idols Bobby Rydell and Bobby Sherman, he was easygoing and full of innocent charm. Others, Gene Vincent and Eddie Cochran among them, tried to emulate Elvis's "hard" side to launch their respective careers.

One Night *(The Burbank Sessions, Vol. I)*

Three versions of "One Night" were performed for the Burbank sessions on June 27, 1968. The first one, from the 6:00 P.M. show, is reviewed here. The Burbank sessions marked the first time since 1961 that Elvis had appeared before a live audience.

The King respected the Beatles' music. Indeed, in his repartee with the audience during the show, the only current musical group he mentions is the Beatles, although he sarcastically follows that with "the Beards," a reference to their hippie style. This is just one hint that Elvis is saying, "No, I am the greatest." He's a fighter on the verge of regaining the world heavyweight championship, as Muhammad Ali later did during the tumultuous times of war and race, peace and protest.

Elvis says during the show, "They're going to let me do what I want . . . ." Throughout the 1960s Elvis was imprisoned behind a wall of retainers and sycophants that he had paid to hide him. And everyone was watching. "One night with you is what I've been praying for" is the knockout punch; the apex of the '68 Burbank sessions.

The King laces "One Night" with lust, for the girl in the song as well as for the audience, whose fresh acceptance he covets. There is such a volatile mix of danger, terror, and euphoria that something has got to give. It does. "Somebody pulled the plug, man," Elvis says, after his guitar cord pops out. The whole room moans, and Elvis slips right back into the beat as if nothing has happened. When he sang the lines "Always lived a very quiet life. . . . *That's been too lonely to long*" earlier in the song, he almost rolled off his seat. Now he's delivering the summation, muscles crouching in his cheeks like snakes, addressing the judge and jury, demanding that the audience believe him. They do.

Jailhouse Rock (*Elvis* [RCA], 1968; *The Burbank Sessions, Vol. I*)

The postage stamp-sized, raised white stage, surrounded by several hundred rabid, mostly female fans, is a canvas that should be hung on a wall in the Smithsonian or the National Gallery. It represents an artistic and historical watershed in Elvis's career, a high ridge bracing the flowing rivers of past and present fervor.

In this performance, following an eloquent interpretation of "Can't Help Falling in Love" the King, dressed in black leather, is a combination of Batman's cool, Spiderman's moves, and Darth Vader's menace. This is a revved-up version of the classic, clocking in at two minutes or so.

"Jailhouse Rock" is clearly the standout performance of the stand-up shows. It is the one song that captures Elvis's release of frustration. He becomes an Omaha Beach invasion, a whirling dervish of fireworks and splashing determination, bending backwards, forwards, sideways, twisting, knee-contorting, then driving the message home in an attempt to dispel the caricatures of his recent past. Unlike the 1950s, in the '60s he has been chained by a carny, contracts, and his own fears. Now he dares to put it all on the line, desperate to succeed and driving to resurrect his image.

The edge of danger is so infused with the joy of dance and song, it's impossible to separate the emotions. Then the audience erupts, clapping and bobbing, as Elvis bends and sways backwards again, almost parallel to the stage, one leg thrust out invitingly, feeling the energy, the words "Let's rock" echoing through the speakers.

♦ ♦ ♦ ♦

Several years ago, Steve Binder related to us that Colonel Tom Parker wanted Elvis to end *The '68 Comeback Special* with "Silent

Night," and then send his best wishes to everyone. Binder and Presley wanted nothing like that. Binder contacted choral director Earl Brown, telling him that he wanted a song that "would blow everyone's mind." Brown and Binder then talked to Elvis about his worldwide social and political views. Brown set the King's thoughts to words and music, resulting in the protest/message song "If I Can Dream."

The next morning, the song was played for Elvis. He eventually listened to it six times—and then he was convinced. "I'll do it," he said. "I'll do it."

When the Colonel heard about this revolt, he was outraged, charging that the only way Elvis would do this song was over Parker's dead body. Elvis overrode the Colonel's tantrums, and the special ended with "If I Can Dream."

The big difference in Elvis's attitude was his interest in and passion for this project. It really mattered to him, and he felt strongly enough about it to stand up to Parker. When Elvis was lazy and uninterested, he often gave in to the Colonel. One final point: In this instance, Elvis had someone (Binder) who would stand with him.

If I Can Dream (*Elvis* [RCA], 1968; *The Burbank Sessions, Vol. 2*)

"If I Can Dream" was inspired by Dr. Martin Luther King Jr.'s "I Have a Dream" speech and the lives and deaths of Dr. King and Robert Kennedy. Elvis sings the swan song of *The '68 Comeback Special* with sanctified soul.

He appears on stage in a white double-breasted suit, buttoned-down, a tie as scarlet as a hibiscus flower. A big red-neon marquee dotted with white lights shouting *ELVIS* hovers behind him. It looks like a Las Vegas set from his '70s club shows or a scene from the 1973 television special *Elvis: Aloha from Hawaii.* The overdubbed horns and female background vocals, sometimes overdone, enhance the scenario.

Yet Elvis seems totally oblivious to all the hoopla. He's in a zone, like Terry Bradshaw in Super Bowl XIII; Michael Jordan in the NBA Finals; Franklin Roosevelt proclaiming, "We have nothing to fear but fear itself"; and Dr. King delivering his "I Have a Dream" speech of 1963: "Now is the time to rise from the dark and desolate valley of segregation to the sunlit path of racial justice."

Looking cool, his hair slicked back, Elvis begins, "There must be lights burning brighter, somewhere." The King is also humble and pious, in stark contrast to the earlier, furious sit-down shows, when he was a coiling, deadly, tropical mamba in a skin-tight black leather suit, his blue eyes slithering through the audience, ready to strike. Closing his eyes while he renders the line "deep in my heart there's a tremblin' . . . question," the rock 'n' holy roller haltingly begins revving up ("Still I am sure that the answer, the answer's gonna come"). Slowly, the rpm's rise, 3,000, 4,000, 5,000 ("There's a beckoning candle, oh yeah" and "while I can think, while I can walk, while I can stand . . . please let my dream come true—right now—oh, let it come true right now"), his right hand rowing back and forth across his body. Elvis is a rebel minister, crying out for action, for change, for peace. Robert Kennedy's favorite and most-used quote was from George Bernard Shaw: "Some men see things as they are and say, why? I dream things that never were and ask, why not?"

This song rivals "How Great Thou Art" in Elvis's vast catalog of gospel tunes. Everything he has ever done is poured into this plea; his body English is restrained yet slightly abandoned; his voice is passionate as a parishioner moving toward the altar to seek the Lord's forgiveness, then calm like a preacher offering reassurance ("the strong winds of promise that will blow away the doubt and fear"), his voice wavering on "fear." This is also a song about Elvis breaking the bonds of his own servitude to fame and fortune ("Tell me why, oh why, oh why, won't that sun appear"), and he sings with his deepest intensity.

Finally, "If I Can Dream" harmonizes "the jangling discord of our nation into a beautiful symphony of brotherhood."

♦ ♦ ♦ ♦

The 1968 sit-down shows of the Burbank sessions comprise the best and richest music of Elvis's career. Even though he sits casually in a chair, as if at a family reunion—which it is—on the intimate stage, the King puts on an unchoreographed, scintillating show. He takes various positions for different songs, jumping, shaking, embodying the music, while his humor and personality are infectious as a child's shenanigans.

Elvis rises to the challenge of *The '68 Comeback Special.* Many critics, including Greil Marcus, attest that the music in the sit-down por-

tions of the show is the greatest rock 'n' roll ever made. Some even believe this is the best concert ever. The drama and richness created by Elvis's voice and guitar playing make this music special. His guitar playing is so dominant that he doesn't need any other instrumental accompaniment. Unfortunately, the best of the sit-down sessions has not been released on a legitimate RCA album.

Below are the best performances from the 6:00 P.M. and 8:00 P.M. shows:

"That's All Right (Mama)"—6:00
"Heartbreak Hotel"—6:00
"Love Me"—6:00
"Blue Suede Shoes"—8:00
"Tiger Man"—8:00
"Are You Lonesome Tonight?"—6:00
"When My Blue Moon Turns to Gold Again"—8:00
"Santa Claus Is Back in Town"—8:00
"Blue Christmas"—8:00
"Lawdy, Miss Clawdy"—8:00
"Tryin' to Get to You"—8:00
"One Night"—6:00
"Baby, What You Want Me to Do"—6:00
"One Night"—6:00
"Memories"—6:00

It is vital that both 6:00 P.M. versions of "One Night" be included for all lovers of rock 'n' roll. We reviewed the first version, but the second "One Night" at 6:00 is also noteworthy in that the King almost recaptures the anthem-like fire of the first "One Night" and is more humorous. It was the second performance of "One Night" at 6:00 that aired on NBC. Elvis did a third take of "One

Night" during the 8:00 sit-down show. The first "One Night" at 6:00 is the best.

"Baby, What You Want Me to Do" was sung by the King three times at the 6:00 sit-down show and twice at the 8:00 sit-down show. The third rendition at 6:00 is by far the best. Elvis reprised this song so often because he and Steve Binder had worked out a plan for these unrehearsed sessions. Whenever Elvis did not know what to do next, he broke into the song for various amounts of time. The second version of "Baby, What You Want Me to Do" at 6:00 aired on NBC.

The NBC show is available on video as *Elvis: The '68 Comeback Special.* There is also a video called *Elvis: One Night with You*, which consists of the 6:00 sit-down show. These are the only legitimate video packages.

One of the most insightful statements ever made about Elvis came from Bono, the lead singer for U2, who said, "Elvis Presley had the kind of wisdom that makes wise men look dumb." Here's an example that might help explain Bono's insight: In the first few numbers of the first 1968 sit-down show, Scotty Moore was, as usual, playing lead guitar. Although Elvis was giving an excellent performance of "That's All Right (Mama)," the King thought something was wrong. So, after a few more songs, he took the lead/electric guitar away from Moore and began playing it himself. This immediately resulted in a marked improvement in Elvis's singing. Commenting on that, producer Steve Binder told us a few years ago, "It freed Elvis, and his guitar playing could not have fit his singing more perfectly."

Elvis's decision in this case says a great deal about his unorthodox genius. He had recorded many of the same songs in the 1950s that he would do that night. However, the King played lead guitar only once in the '50s, on "One Night with You."

Why would Elvis, with his career on the line in this *Comeback Special*, take such a risk? Even with Scotty Moore playing lead, Elvis was singing superbly. It was the musical equivalent of Muhammad Ali employing the now-famous "rope-a-dope" strategy to reclaim the heavyweight championship of the world from George Foreman.

What appeared to be suicidal was, in fact, inspired. Steve Binder related that Elvis's confidence had grown during his early dressing-room-area jam sessions, in which he sometimes played lead guitar. Nonetheless, to actually do it with his career on the line was outrageous. All the "experts" thought Ali was committing suicide when he lay on the ropes, round after round, letting Foreman pound away until he was so exhausted that Ali was easily able to knock out the bigger man and reclaim the title. The same reaction from the "experts" should have greeted Elvis when he took over lead guitar, but no one had a chance to ponder his strategy in advance—he just did it, proving that he, indeed, possessed the "wisdom that makes wise men look dumb."

Like Ali's bold rope-a-dope idea, Elvis's move of taking over the electric guitar makes perfect sense—in hindsight. Moore's playing resembled, almost exactly, the way he had played in the '50s; but Elvis sang quite differently than he had earlier in his career. Scotty's playing did not live up to Elvis's passion and his determination to reinvent himself, and it forced the King to work within limitations, compromising his passion. Greil Marcus eloquently observes that, when Elvis took over the lead/electric guitar, he led the music and took us into a new world.

When Elvis made this move, he gained the freedom necessary for full expression. The chords were simple, but as Marcus avers, "You can live a dozen lifetimes and not get that sound." It is furious, dangerous, filled with fire; Elvis stamps his personality all over the guitar like a designer's logo. To experience the difference between the two guitar styles, just listen to songs from the Sun sessions and the 1968 sit-down performance, back to back. Compared to the fury of the latter, the Sun renditions seem like lullabies.

Greil Marcus, writing about the 1968 sit-down shows, observes

that "Elvis gives us a metaphor for the possibilities of life, a metaphor that's so rich it makes almost every job, all love stories, all religious experiences, almost every presidential candidate . . . except Roosevelt seem like a terrible compromise. I leave out Roosevelt because I heard some of his 1936 campaign speeches, and they had just the kind of drama, just the kind of humor I found here."

NBC and RCA strongly promoted *The '68 Comeback Special.* After the network and record company executives saw tapes of the show, they resolved that if Presleymania were going to happen again, they weren't going to miss out on it. The promotional clips fed to the networks whetted the audience's appetite for more.

The show aired Tuesday night, December 3, at 9 P.M. Eastern and destroyed the formidable competition: *Red Skelton* and *Doris Day* on CBS and *It Takes a Thief* and *NYPD* on ABC. In fact, the special was the top-rated program of the year. When NBC rebroadcast the program in August, it received another stunningly high rating.

Reviews of the *Comeback Special* gushed with unstinting praise. The King had returned.

CHAPTER 5

The Memphis Sessions: Sweet Soulful Music

Elvis Presley followed the 1968 Burbank sessions with some of the greatest singing of his career in what are now known as the "Memphis sessions."

Unless otherwise specified, the songs discussed in this chapter can be found on the *From Elvis in Memphis* album, CD, or cassette. Do *not* get *The Memphis Sessions* album, for it was tampered with instrumentally by RCA.

During these sessions, Elvis wove an intricate tapestry of thoughtfulness, insight, biker-bar toughness, and savvy—tempered by *Grand Ole Opry* delicacy and seasoned with romantic aplomb—to conceive an album that goes beyond a specific genre or concept. From country to blues to rock to ballad reconfigurations, the Memphis sessions represent a sophisticated extension of Elvis's roots. Many other songs were recorded at these sessions, but we have reviewed only those that are most representative of the music's complexity and range.

With the success of *The '68 Comeback Special* behind him, Elvis approached the Memphis sessions with a confidence and enthusiasm that he had not exhibited in the studio since the 1950s, according to friends. The zestfulness he felt about his life and career was contagious. He was dividing his time between Memphis and Hollywood, and was socializing more and more. That was always a good sign. When Elvis withdrew to Graceland, he was in trouble. Before the cold weather hit Memphis in January 1969, the King could often be seen riding horses and mingling outdoors with friends and fans, according to Jerry Schilling and others.

Wearin' that Loved On Look

This is the perfect song to open the *From Elvis in Memphis* album. It's tough and aggressive, with no frills or nonsense. Elvis's voice is raw, rough, and working-class, and the "baby" vocal and chorus are reminiscent of Eric Burdon on "It's My Life," the Animals' best song. Each musician supports Elvis well, for different sidemen are spotlighted as the song proceeds. They are all asked to keep up with the King, who does many remarkable things with his voice, painting chiaroscuro images and playing innocently yet forcefully off the Motown-style "shoop" backup vocals.

The most notable thing about this song is that Elvis sings with real balls. Perhaps the only other white men of the period who could sing with such brashness were Tom Jones and Jerry Lee Lewis, but Elvis's interpretations were usually more layered and complex than theirs. "Loved On Look" is steamy crotch rock at its best.

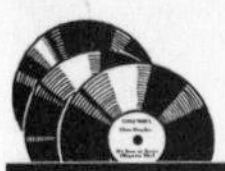

Only the Strong Survive

It takes guts to cover Jerry Butler's superb original of this song, but that is what it's about, after all. This is one of many songs written about a mother's advice, such as the Miracles' "Shop Around" and the Shirelles' "Mama Said," and the King understands its importance. Of particular note is the narrative that starts "I remember my first love affair, somehow or another, the whole damn thing went wrong," conveying the mixed emotions of a man who is trying to be strong but has not yet reached that point, and the confusion and pain of the jilted lover. It's a fine piece of acting, matched by delicate singing of the mama's role ("There's gonna be a whole lotta trouble in your life . . .") and gathering courage in the refrain ("You gotta be a man, you gotta take a stand").

The music is adroitly balanced to the varying moods Elvis displays. Gene Chrisman's drums and Reggie Young's guitar are sharp and crisp when the beat picks up, restrained yet supportive during the storytelling. The string section harmonizes rather than taking the lead, which would have been tempting but deadly. This is mature music-making of a highly respectable caliber.

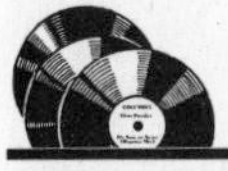

I'll Hold You in My Heart (Till I Hold You in My Arms)

In this erotic fantasy, Elvis's elocution always maintains a sharp edge at the right moments, like a sliver of distant golden lightning disturbing a dream. His phrasing, use of the microphone (somehow making popping sounds, as if plugging into a high-voltage electrical

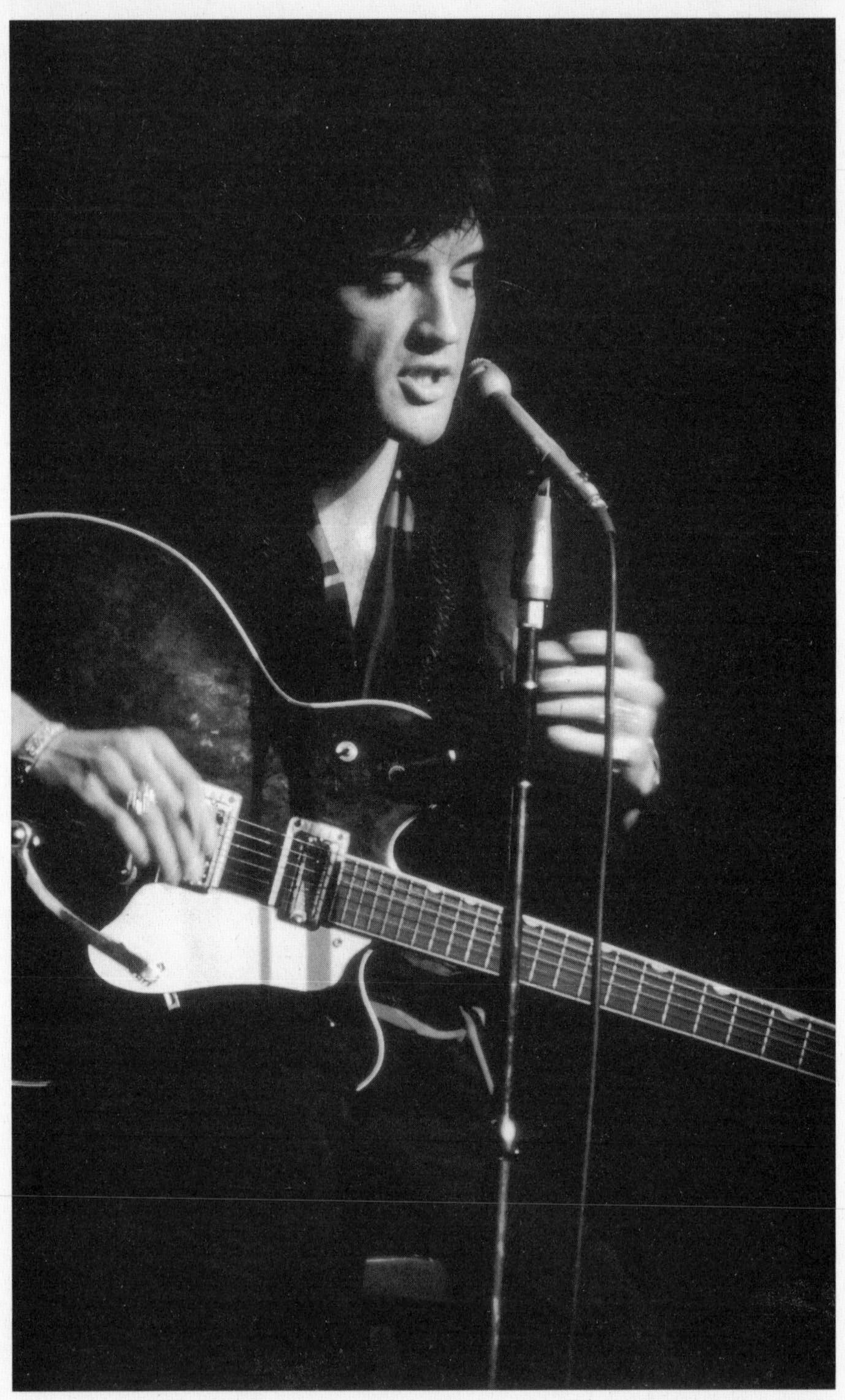

socket), and piano playing combine with the excellent support provided by guitar and drums to enhance the drama. The basic accompaniment is a crucial choice. The production and arrangement are not intrusive but rather promote subtle encouragement. Although the lyrics seem to be unimportant and repetitive, there is a sublime soulfulness here, and the simple words and phrases contribute to the obsessive quality of the performance.

Elvis is entrapped by the music, while at the same time breaking out through the back door and setting off the house alarm system. When he repeats "I'm away, I'm away . . . from you" in the second chorus, fear and longing are so fused together that it's difficult to tell them apart. Elvis is so focused on the song that a hurricane could blow the roof off the studio, but he would still be sitting at the piano, playing and singing to the roiling sky.

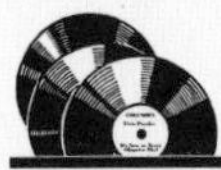

Long Black Limousine

In the words of Elvis biographer and rock critic Peter Guralnick, "Elvis transforms a fairly ordinary song into a vehicle of savage social protest," as he vehemently rebels against the woman's life style and the cultural paradigms that blind her. The opening, with a tolling bell, piano, and drumsticks, creates a feeling of foreboding. The tolling bell, a cliché with lesser artists, punctuates Elvis's bitterness even while it softens his delivery into sadness before he launches into the body of the song. The backup singers rally around his diatribe against social ascendancy—and the people who choose it at the expense of love.

This is a "Poor Side of Town" that Johnny Rivers dares not touch, as sweet as the song is. "Long Black Limousine" could have been directed by Martin Scorsese. When Elvis sings, "you finally had your dream," we can almost see him fondling a .357 Magnum, then shoving it back into his leather holster.

One point should be noted about the *From Elvis in Memphis* album: Before Elvis got hold of these songs, many of them were ordinary or below average, with little appeal. Elvis transformed them, raising them to such a level that, in the words of Greil Marcus, "There are no weak spots on the album."

Chips Moman, who produced sessions for many artists, including Dusty Springfield and Neil Diamond, produced the Memphis sessions. Moman, the Thomas Street Band (the studio house band), and mostly Elvis Presley turned some of these cuts into excellent records. But even the King couldn't make the worst of this lot into high-caliber material. Examples are "I'm Movin' On," "True Love Travels on a Gravel Road," and "Power of My Love," although all are respectable tracks. Covering many musical genres, Elvis elevates his vocal prowess on *From Elvis in Memphis*.

Gentle On My Mind

This song has always been so bizarre: a concoction of smooth country and spaced-out lyrics worthy of late-'60s psychedelia at its peak. Dig these lines: "I dipped my cup of soup from a gurglin', cracklin' cauldron in some train yard." Yeah, Jim Morrison took a hit after getting off the blue bus at Moonlight Drive. Or maybe this is really an outtake from Black Sabbath's 1971 heavy metal Godfather, *Paranoid*. Nevertheless, it's always been strictly middle-of-the-road fare by various artists, a big hit for Glen Campbell.

Elvis rides with the words "my sleeping bag rolled up and stashed behind your couch." This is another strange druggie line—where did he sleep; what was the nature of their relationship? We don't know for sure, and we never will. Elvis communicates the lost, desperate reveries of a truly homeless man ("Through cupped hands 'round a tin can, I pretend to hold you to my breast") with a voice forlorn as a panhandler begging spare change at the entrance to Burger King. Elvis plunks down at the edge of an alleyway, water running toward a drain, people rushing by, while she's "wavin' from the back roads of the rivers of my memory."

It's impossible to get a feel for this song until you hear the King create this wandering drifter. The synthesizer effects really take it over the top, a guitar pick wedged into the intake valve of a broken-down semi. It's ready to roll again, and Elvis has a ticket back to Memphis.

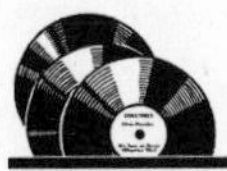

Movin' On

This song is a Hank Snow truck-drivin', woman-losin' ditty, sung with fast-talkin' high intensity, as if Elvis were addressing a whole convoy of female flames over the CB radio. Breaker one-nine, there's a Smokey at Exit 9, you copy? The King is truly a method actor here (he drove a truck in his youth) and delivers this vocal as smoothly as an eighteen-wheeler chasing a Chevy Cavalier down a two-lane Tennessee highway, headlights flashing on and off. Get outa my way, baby!

Chips Moman's Thomas Street Band provides steller supplementary sound effects. The guitar intro is a direct rip-off of the incomparable Keith Richards's taunting opening notes to the Rolling Stones' "Off the Hook" from *12 x 5*, plucky yet played slowly, pistons at a clean idle. Then "Movin' On" works its way quickly through all the gears, shifting the stick, punching the clutch, faster than Bad Company's different song with the same name. John Hughey's steel guitar fades in and out like a train in the mountains, while the horn section blows hard as a big Mack truck's warning. Mike Leech's constant, prickly pickin' bass lines punctuate the attitude: "Your true lovin' daddy, he ain't comin back—keep movin' on . . . rattling free." No red lights flashing in the rearview mirror, no sirens for at least a hundred miles.

Moman's tendency to overorchestrate is a hindrance at times, but this is a decent record, nonetheless.

True Love Travels a Gravel Road

Revelation 21:4 states, "He shall wipe every tear from their eyes, and there shall be no more death or mourning." Elvis sings, with perfectly timed tambourine and trap-drum encouragement, "down through the years, we've had hard times and tears, but they only helped our love grow." "True Love Travels" is steeped with the King's gospel influences, but it is also dramatically tinged with the blues and pop. The guitar sounds like a slow, Bluesbreakers Eric Clapton, and when Elvis praises "not once have I seen your blue eyes fill with envy," the melody is stone-cold Roy Orbison in "Crying" ("the touch of your hand makes me stop and say hello"). Elvis's "We'll stay together no matter how strong the wind blows" contains standard pop sentiments that can also be heard on such songs as the Beach Boys' "Don't Worry, Baby" and the Crystals' "Uptown."

The King's vocal intonations manipulate the lyrics deftly, as if he's somewhere deep in the Appalachians where love survives, while "hearts are in danger on smooth streets paved with gold." Yeah, this is a country song, too. These eclectic qualities are impressive, but "True Love Travels" is only a fair song and a mediocre production.

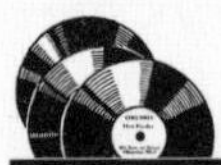

Any Day Now

This song is a good illustration of why Chips Moman is not considered one of the great producers of the rock 'n' roll era. The loud, overdone orchestration does its best to ruin this passable song. One does not usually expect passion and overt sexual yearning from a Burt Bacharach tune, although exceptions include Dionne Warwick's "Anyone Who Had a Heart" and this sensitively horny recording by Elvis.

It is Elvis's poignant longing that makes this song go. The band opens urgently, lead guitar up-tempo, strong rhythm guitar synchronizing with the muted string section like an amber light flashing at a crossroads after midnight. This warning, smoldering sound marks the rhythm playing throughout—hesitant, yet forceful. The horns kick in briefly, a young mare whinnying in her stall. The line "Any day now . . . my wild beautiful bird, you will have flown . . . I'll be alone" demonstrates Elvis's anxiety. He sings confidently, however, briefly taunting that she will never find a lover as lusty as he ("Any day now, love will let you down . . . whoa, whoa"), then follows with a sweet vocal and musical passage ("Until you're gone forever, I'll be holding on for dear life"). He sings the last word as if he doesn't want to let it go, at the edge of tears.

At the end, the listener is sure that her other lover "won't be around." The fading, layered finale ("Don't fly away") is not destroyed by the overzealous production.

Power of My Love

Chips Moman is at it again: overproducing a song and not turning Elvis's voice up to the level it should be. As powerfully as the King sings this song, it is probably the weakest cut on *From Elvis in Memphis*. Potentially one of the album's better songs, "Power" starts intriguingly with the catchy lyrics ("Oh break it, burn it, drag it all around"), sung with tai chi precision to the accompaniment of a menacing, slow blues guitar and a solid rhythm section. Then the over-charted horns blast into the mix like a group of Hell's Angels and "crush it, kick it" nearly to death. The tough line "Baby, you can't lick it, huh, I'll make you give in" sounds muddled, like a man trying to talk to his lover at the corner of Fifth and Main during rush hour.

Elvis does the best he can, but many of the intricacies of his performance—as well as those of the core Thomas Street Band and singers—are lost. This recording can't seem to decide whether its role model should be a numbingly brassy number by Chicago or a cool John Lee Hooker tune. It's quite frustrating because the next-to-last verse ("pound it, ah, what good does it do") returns to the power of the intro and is set up by some sexy moaning by the female chorus. However, the horns are overly plentiful and detrimental to the groovy, repeated refrain that closes the cut ("Every hour you'll be shaken by the strength and the power . . .").

At least there are no violins!

It Keeps Right on a Hurtin'

A very wise addition to *From Elvis in Memphis*, this Johnny Tillotson song gives the album a nice change of pace, tempering its intensity with a smooth, country/pop groove. Tillotson had a big crossover hit with a "teen" rendition of this song, his naturally higher voice mimicking, at times, '50s doo-wop standards. Elvis, in his mid-30s now, flirts with higher registers but deliberately pulls back at just the right times ("I can't help it, I don't think I can go on"). The vibrato in his voice threatens to reach a loftier pitch with the last word, "onnn," but instead chooses to relay a deeper, more mature sense of loss and passion, a reflective realization of aloneness. The line "the pillow where you laid your head now holds my empty dreams" is sung against hypnotic background percussion.

Elvis still can't quite believe it, despite crying "a billion tears," as he stares down from the seventh floor of some fancy hotel after midnight, between gigs, at a couple embracing in the center of the swimming pool, then joyously splashing water over empty lounge chairs. But there's no envy nor self-pity, only acceptance of what he can't change, as he smiles and turns away from the window.

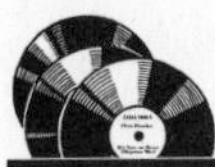

After Lovin' You

This song is a struggle between healing salve ("your memory you know, it will remain") and torn bandages ("I'm no good, I'm no good, ah, to anyone"). An inspired blues recollection piece that can trace its roots to the various versions of "One Night"(especially the 1968 rendition), "After Lovin' You" takes us to the deep recesses of mourning, where hope and possibility are pinned against the basement wall like an old dart board, warped and pock-marked.

Remember the 1961 doo-wop classic "My True Story" by the Jive Five? The lugubrious beat and rhythm are the same here, but Elvis's vocals don't "cry cry cry," as Eugene Pitt's do. They crawl, stumble, and growl for release from memories ("Ah, I know I'll go through life comparing her to you"). This is an abandoned cat clawing at the cellar window, knowing he can't get back in ("Another love may come along, they can't live up to you"). Elvis is raw, intense, and spirited, galvanized at least as much by the bluesy sound as by the lyrics.

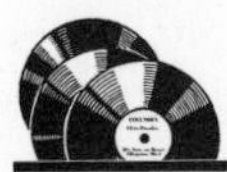

In the Ghetto

For years we thought Elvis's singing of this song was no better than good. It wasn't until we heard his version of "In the Ghetto" on the

Lost Performances video that we became attuned to just how understated yet indelible his vocalizations on the Memphis sessions are. The King sings with controlled desperation, all the while delicately enunciating key words and phrases.

When not using tonality to enhance the impact of certain words, Elvis's studio-attuned voice takes on the tenor of shivering reality. The version of "In the Ghetto" that emerged from the Memphis sessions is definitely a mood piece. In some instances, Elvis's voice lingers on a word, a soft breeze rippling the waters. When he sings, "And his hunger burns," Elvis's haunting tone on the word "burns" echoes with layered meanings, foreshadowing the tragedy of a boy's death in the street, embodying the present injustice.

"In the Ghetto" is also one of Moman's best production efforts, from the mournful backup vocals (which, according to the book *Recording Sessions* by Ernst Jorgensen, Erik Rasmussen, and Johnny Mikkelsen, Elvis insisted upon using) to the methodical, military funeral-style drumming at the end. This song combines religious fervor with political/social consciousness, and Elvis executes it with mature wisdom and grace.

Elvis isn't just describing a forelorn condition, as most protest singers do; he is urging others to become involved. Tragically, "In the Ghetto" is perhaps as relevant today as it was when it was released.

Two sources who wish to remain unidentified told us that Colonel Tom Parker made a fuss about Elvis cutting "In the Ghetto." He objected to the King making message songs and delving into social protest material. Just as Elvis had held his ground regarding their conflicts over *The '68 Comeback Special*, he affirmed that, when it came to music, the final choice was his own.

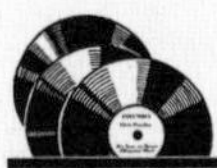

Rubberneckin' (*Collector's Gold,* 1991)

There were two versions of this average rocker recorded in 1969. The first featured the Thomas Street Band at the Memphis sessions, and the second was a live cut with Elvis's new band. The latter group, led by James Burton and backed by the Sweet Inspirations, was an outstanding rock ensemble—clearly superior to Chips Moman's aggregation—and is showcased on *Collector's Gold.*

The Memphis track is sharp and clean, with the Thomas Street Band in a rockin' groove that never overpowers the precise interplay between Elvis and the supporting singers' voices. It also includes the verse ". . . I look, stand everywhere, and I see everything in sight," which is missing on the live rendition, and adds punch to the "stop, look and listen, baby" refrain.

The quicker tempo and almost wild synchronicity of the live performance is more appropriate for the robust, freewheeling character Elvis portrays. The rhythm section and Burton's burning guitar nearly run the song off the road, sliding through the sharp turns, but this racer stays on course ("I like what I see, I see what I like. Yeah, it gives me such a blow . . . ho ho, yeah yeah!") until the final "Stop!" If "Rubberneckin' " had been recorded in the early 1960s, it could have started a new dance craze.

Despite the contributions of the new live band and Elvis's macho panache, "Rubberneckin' " is still a little too hefty and struts a bit too hard.

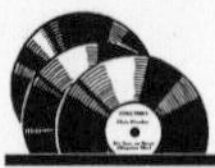

Kentucky Rain *(Elvis: Worldwide 50 Gold Award Hits, Vol. 1, 1970)*

This song is both simple and complex, suffused with feelings rich as spring in Bluegrass country. Elvis gives an intelligent and moving performance on this challenging number, using his vocal modulations to full advantage in capturing the song's variety of sentiments. He creates a vivid atmosphere for listeners, painting pictures of his bewildered, chilly, and wet journey.

The chorus ("and up ahead, another town that I've been walkin' through, with the rain in my shoes, searching for you") is superlative singing. Elvis condenses the pining, frustration, realization, and hope that all love affairs contain into a short story that improves with every listening.

This "cold, dark afternoon" is transformed into "a prayer that I'd find you," although "Kentucky Rain" ends while the storm continues.

"Suspicious Minds" was first released by its writer, Mark James, but it went nowhere on the charts. It was a very different song when sung by Elvis Presley, produced by Chips Moman, and played by the Thomas Street Band. Marty Lacker of the Memphis Mafia arranged for Elvis to record it at American Studios. He affirmed to us that practically everyone present in the studio believed that this was a can't-miss number-one hit.

A problem erupted, however, and guess who instigated it? Colonel Thomas Andrew Parker. Lacker relates that it wasn't the song the Colonel objected to, it was the royalty distributions. This was typical of Parker; he wanted to throw away the greatest song Elvis had been given to record in years because he (Parker) was not getting all he wanted in terms of profit. The Colonel thought he would prevail in this, for while Elvis decided what music he would record, the business aspects of the King's career were entirely in Parker's domain.

No way! Nothing was going to stop Elvis from recording this song. It even reached the point where Mark James was walking out of the studio, but Elvis stopped him. The King was adamant and persistent about recording "Suspicious Minds," and he straightened out the problem by himself. The Colonel was surprised by the determination of the man he spoke of as "my boy."

Suspicious Minds *(Elvis's Greatest Hits, 1981)*

This song is about Shakespeare's "green-eyed monster," jealousy—only this time the lady (Desdemona), not Othello, is the obsessed character. The bubbling bass and the offbeat, punctuating fuzz tone of the saxophone give the record a distinct flavor. In addition, the strings, brass, guitar, drums, and chorus join together seamlessly as the song builds to its climax, much like a Phil Spector Wall of Sound gem. This is blue-eyed soul rock 'n' roll, with the hot touch of a torch song. The passion and sensitivity are absent when others attempt to sing "Suspicious Minds," but when Elvis performs it, the jealous lady's paranoia becomes contagious.

The King rocks with the song while infusing it with numerous musical styles, including his own synthesis. He captures the suspicion, entrapment, and betrayal of love, yet also communicates a forgiveness and an almost unbearable gentleness of spirit. At the end, Elvis is still "caught in a trap," but he's not giving up. He conducts a double cross-examination of her and himself that results in a new awareness but without resolution. Still, Elvis somehow reaches a state of euphoria in this record.

"Suspicious Minds" is to the Memphis sessions what "Mystery Train" is to the Sun sessions. Each is the best cut of its respective session, and each features a sustained inquiry into love's intensity. Elvis received much praise for the singles and the *From Elvis in Memphis* album, which Dave Marsh calls a "masterpiece."

The King wanted to prove that he could make a modern conceptual album, the kind that the Beatles, Bob Dylan, the Rolling Stones and the Who had done so successfully. Despite some production flaws, the songs here are thematically and musically linked in the most fundamental ways. As Dave Marsh wrote in his book *Elvis*, "Very little of what Elvis recorded in Memphis is pure rock 'n' roll; none of it is straight blues. Yet all of the tracks derive their sense of aggression from rock, and their groove is inevitably born of the blues. The very best tracks are quite beyond genre."

Elvis was in great voice for the Memphis sessions. The rawness and the growling was the result of his singing from the gut—not his voice cracking. Elvis never again sounded like this because, after once more conquering the music world with the Memphis sessions, he never again had the same hunger to reach beyond himself.

From Elvis in Memphis contains the darkest images of anything Elvis ever recorded. He takes us on a mysterious ride through hidden backstreets and lonely vistas of the soul and heart but makes us rely on him to get us home safely.

With all that *From Elvis in Memphis* has to offer, it must be remembered that the two greatest cuts from the Memphis sessions, "Suspicious Minds" and "Kentucky Rain," were not even included on the LP. Such was the custom at the time but not any more. Since singles sales carry so little weight, all of the best cuts from sessions today are put on albums. This includes all the major chart-toppers: Michael Jackson's *Thriller*, Springsteen's *Born in the U.S.A.*, etc. So, if "Suspicious Minds" and "Kentucky Rain" had been included on *From Elvis in Memphis*, the album would have garnered even more critical praise.

♦ ♦ ♦ ♦

Elvis would follow these recordings with the finest concerts of his career in August 1969 at the International Hotel in Las Vegas. His Madison Square Garden and *Aloha from Hawaii* concerts were pathetic compromises compared to the 1969 Vegas shows. Even the eminent concerts of 1970 pale next to these. Although the music was better in the sit-down portion of *The '68 Comeback Special*, the overall impact of the 1969 Las Vegas performances was significantly higher.

Let's talk a little about Elvis's voice—the instrument itself. In his book, *The Great American Popular Singer,* Henry Pleasants describes the technical qualities of the King's voice in this way:

> Elvis's voice covers about two octaves and a third, from the baritone's low G to the tenor's high B, with an upward extension in falsetto to at least a D-flat.
>
> His best octave is the middle, granting an extra full step either up or down. . . . In ballads and country songs he belts out full-voiced high G's and A's that an opera baritone might envy. [No other single artist has] influenced the course of popular music so profoundly.

Andrew Solt puts it more succinctly when he comments that "Elvis Presley had the greatest voice of the 20th century."

But while a great voice is surely important, that alone will not move us. Phil Gelormine of *Billboard* wrote about that in the very first issue of the original *Elvis World*:

> I have seen them all; from Crosby to Como, Sinatra to the Beatles, and Dylan to the Stones. But friends, I can honestly assure you without a doubt, *you have picked the best*! I am of the opinion that Elvis Presley was the most gifted singer of our time. He had

> an inborn *feel* of music like that of no other vocalist I have listened to. Elvis Presley left a tremendous legacy of varied music for the world to enjoy. And that voice . . . that majestic Southern baritone which was filled with such vivid color, exciting subtlety, and a thousand nuances will be heard for as long as man and machine exist.

Phil Spector, by far the greatest producer of rock 'n' roll records, says this about Elvis:

> Gosh, he's so great. You have no idea how great he is, really you don't. You have no comprehension—it's absolutely impossible. I can't tell you why he's so great, but he is. He's sensational. He can do anything with his voice. He can sing anything you want him to, anyway you tell him. The unquestionable King of rock 'n' roll.

In terms of range, Elvis could sing rock, blues, gospel, country and western, r&b, soul, folk, pop, standards, and ballads with authority. Many rock critics and musicans don't give Elvis credit for this because all they are concerned with is rock 'n' roll.

During the 1969 shows at Las Vegas' International Hotel, Elvis was at his peak in almost every way. According to bodyguards Red and Sonny West, the King was "handsomer than 10 movie stars." He was witty, charming, intellectually acute, and he was functioning on natural energy, free of drugs. Elvis was in the best shape of his career, and he worked out by practicing karate and running.

The show-business bible, *Variety*, reveals that the King's concerts broke all Las Vegas attendance records. Even the great Barbra Streisand couldn't fill the auditorium night after night for a month straight. Vegas veterans report that Elvis's shows at the International were attended by more celebrities than were any other shows in the city's history; indeed, half the seats on opening night were filled by celebrities, critics, and other invited guests.

Gossip columnist May Mann said there were more wet seats for the Elvis engagement that for any other that she had covered. She and other Las Vegas pros believe that a large number of celebrities and fans approached Elvis (mostly for sex) during his shows at the International. For example, ex-Elvis lover Joyce Bova notes in her book, *My Love Affair With Elvis*, that after one of the performances, the King was backstage, greeting fans, when a stunningly beautiful blonde walked into the room. Without missing a stride, she walked slinkily up to Elvis and sat beside him. The blonde was none other than French actress Catherine Deneuve, who was generally acknowledged as the most beautiful woman in the world. She and Elvis talked briefly, and then she popped the proposal, "Let's have sex." Elvis was polite but declined the invitation. Deneuve said, "When you offer yourself, you offer the best that you have," then graciously got up and left the room. Why did Elvis Presley refuse the most beautiful woman in the world? The probable reason was that she was much too forward for him.

After the success of Elvis's 1969 engagement in Las Vegas, Colonel Parker proved that, even where making money was concerned, he had lost his touch. Rock writers Roy Carr and Mick Farran uncovered the story of how Parker loved long-term contracts and negotiated a five-year deal with the International Hotel (later the Las Vegas Hilton). When he inked the contract, Elvis was the highest-paid entertainer in Vegas, but Parker hadn't considered inflation or the fact that salaries were always increasing in the town. So, in the last years of the agreement, three or four entertainers in Las Vegas were making more than Elvis—even though Elvis was a much bigger draw.

Parker may also have signed Elvis's death warrant, for the contract called for the singer to appear in Las Vegas two months a year, doing two shows a night. Two shows in one evening is fine for most

Las Vegas performers—they barely break a sweat. Elvis, on the other hand, melted off nine pounds a night in 1969. The physical and emotional pace was way too much for him and hampered the King's ability to resist chemical assistance. The reason Elvis went along with this was that in 1969, he was so psyched to perform that he thought the feeling would never diminish.

The only outstanding asset the Colonel had left was the air of mystery he and Elvis generated around the King's persona. Elvis would do no interviews or commercials and very little television. Today, even some of the biggest performers are so overexposed that audiences tire of seeing them. For Priscilla Presley to lavish praise on Colonel Tom Parker after his death is, at best, regrettable.

With his return to live performing at the International Hotel, Elvis's comeback was complete. Nevertheless, his ambition was primed, and he wanted the shows to be filmed. First, however, the Colonel decided to do another live album, featuring the King singing other people's songs. Elvis was successful in these performance and the album, *February 1970 On Stage*, was worthwhile.

Elvis felt contentment, since the first three parts of his comeback had been successful. He was outgoing and enjoying life, according to the many friends of the King we interviewed. Priscilla had become one of the most beautiful women in the world, and a baby couldn't be much cuter that Lisa Marie.

CHAPTER 6

The Early Seventies: Sparks of Brilliance, Glimpses of the Fall

According to members of the Memphis Mafia, 1970 was also a good year for Elvis Presley. The television special, the recording session, and his return to live concerts left him feeling fulfilled but anticipating more, like a young fighter, fresh from a knockout victory, staring down his next opponent: February live performances in Las Vegas. Following that engagement, the King would perform six sold-out concerts at the Houston Astrodome, attracting 44,000 fans for each show. He was really looking forward to having his August 1970 performances in Las Vegas filmed for posterity. The director and assistant director of the film, Denis Sanders and John Wilson, confirm that Elvis felt confident about the shows.

By 1971, however, Elvis experienced a radical change for the worse. He had accomplished everything he wanted, with the exception of a world tour and a great movie role, but those were not on the horizon. The King felt discontented and disengaged from meaningful purpose. His drug-taking increased alarmingly, and he began to put on weight. Nineteen seventy-one was really the beginning of Elvis

Presley's downfall. As the bodyguards have claimed, it was the King's fall from grace that pushed Priscilla to ask for a divorce.

By the '70s, except for his live performances, Elvis was no longer interested in producing his own music. Although Elvis always had the final say, Felton Jarvis did the producing. Most of the records were poorly made, often with far too much orchestration. There are exceptions, and some are rockers; "Burning Love" and "Promised Land" are superbly produced. "T-R-O-U-B-L-E" is also well-produced, while the production on "Moody Blue" is acceptable.

Elvis again proved his prowess in live performances, including the Las Vegas shows in February and August 1970, American tours in September and November 1970, and, to a lesser extent, concerts in Boston and Baltimore in 1971, and at New York's Madison Square Garden in June 1972. With each succeeding year, Elvis's concerts became less effective, revealing glimpses of darkness.

The 1970 concert documentary *Elvis: That's the Way It Is* features outstanding work by the King. Some critics have not praised the film because it is not a full-blown rock 'n' roll vehicle. However, there is rousing rock here ("You've Lost that Lovin' Feeling," "Polk Salad Annie," "Suspicious Minds"), but the format of the film is middle-of-the-road. Many mainstream critics and even film experts have recognized the eclectic, probing yet entertaining qualities of *Elvis: That's the Way It Is*. The documentary is not filmed nor edited particularly well, with fan interviews spliced between songs and interfering, but the King's performance is outstanding.

♦ ♦ ♦ ♦

The Wonder of You *(February 1970 On Stage, 1970)*

It's the wonder of Elvis's performance that makes this a bountiful ballad. Recorded live in February 1970, there are several features that stand out. James Burton propels the building emotion with his understated, sensuous guitar work. Just before the instrumental break, Elvis says with anticipation, "Play it, James." There's true respect between the artists—one can feel it. After a few romantic piano notes, James plays a 15-second lead riff, delicate and lovely as a first kiss. It is equal to George Harrison's searching solo on "Something," from *Abbey Road*. The Sweet Inspirations provide provocative background vocals, even during the break. Their "ah ah ah ahs" are enchanting, reminiscent of the Ray Charles Singers on "I Can't Stop Loving You," and Elvis joins in, inspired by the seductive, gospel-influenced chorus. When Elvis sings over the melody, he stencils a beautiful shading on love's silkscreen.

The Sweet Inspirations were the best backup singers ever to perform with Elvis, and the group improved when high-voiced singer Kathy Westmoreland joined Elvis in August 1970. The worst backup ensemble may have been J. D. Sumner and the Stamps Quartet; Elvis often permitted Sumner's low, maudlin voice to suck the life out of a song. Of course, the Jordanaires were perfect for Elvis's '50s music, but the Sweet Inspirations rank with some of the better female groups in rock 'n' roll.

The richness of Elvis's voice ("I guess I'll never know the reason why you love me as you do—that's the wonder, the wonder of you") is a combination of shy reverence and bold, honest appreciation of this woman, which spurred many people to become Elvis fans. He sings the song as a projection of what love should be—and what it can feel like to everyone.

"The Wonder of You" is also featured on the videotape *Elvis: The Lost Performances*, but that version lacks the energy and inspiration that has made the February 1970 take one of the King's finest love songs. Elvis's husky, majestic sound on "The Wonder of You" has been copied by many middle-of-the-road performers.

Finally, as evidenced by this song and so many others, Elvis leads his band. The King is also a maestro.

♦ ♦ ♦ ♦

Following the release of the *February 1970 On Stage* and *That's the Way It Is* albums in 1970, we believe Elvis became convinced that he had reached his peak as a ballad singer. Most of the songs on these albums are straight ballads, unlike the rock ballads on *From Elvis in Memphis*, and the King's performances showcase a maturity that is absent from the material he recorded prior to *The '68 Comeback Special*. Elvis always wanted to be respected as an articulate singer of standards, and now he was.

These are not soul ballads; Elvis just lets his feelings flow with the right combination of ease and intensity—these are torch songs, love songs. Elvis had recorded many fine ballads before—"Love Me Tender" and "Can't Help Falling in Love," for example—but now he had more life experiences to tap and had finely tuned the technique demanded by the traditional musical form.

"The Wonder of You," "Let It Be Me," "I've Lost You," "I Just Can't Help Believin' " and "The Next Step Is Love" are among his most accomplished ballad performances. There were other ballads from that time period—"Stranger in the Crowd" and "Just Pretend"—that didn't make the grade because of overorchestration and Elvis's lack of creativity. They sounded too much like Engelbert Humperdinck, playing the Vegas craps game to the bitter end.

Elvis's emergence as a fully developed ballad singer is something he had been working on since the 1950s. In later years, the King would hit higher notes, but with the exception of a few performances, they were not delivered with the same care that his best ballads of the early '70s were.

♦ ♦ ♦ ♦

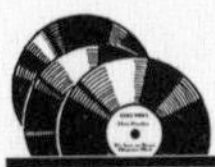

Polk Salad Annie (*That's the Way It Is* video, 1970; a different but equally intuitive version can be heard on *February 1970 On Stage,* 1970)

The August 1970 concert at Las Vegas' International Hotel provides a finger-lickin' good performance of "Polk Salad" for the King's *That's the Way It Is* video. Elvis and the band let the song build heat and humidity like a summer day on the bayou. A brief, memorable portrait of a girl with nothing left to lose is played loose and rowdy, with Elvis struttin', shakin', and scattin' as if he has swamp fever. He really seems to enjoy telling the story ("A mean, vicious, straight-razor totin' woman, Lord have mercy").

At one point, Elvis sticks the microphone into his mouth and mumbles for a few moments. He often joked around like this to keep the drama of a song from becoming too intense. The band, particularly drummer Ronnie Tutt and guitarist James Burton, becomes infected by Elvis's daring improvisations—at least three new dance steps are invented here!—and they're stirrin' up a big batch of greens in a boiling pot. Burton's whirling wah-wah guitar almost spins out of control as it keeps pace with Elvis's "Sock a little polk salad" dance and vocal wizardry. The King twirls his right arm over his head like a lariat, while the Sweet Inspirations' "chick a boom" chorus chops hot peppers into the mix. If you've never seen this video, rent it tonight!

I've Lost You (*Elvis: The Other Sides; Worldwide Gold Award Hits, Vol. 2,* 1971)

This often neglected gem was written by Howard-Blaikley in the midst of the King's late 1960s to early '70s comeback period with a full-fledged band, orchestration, and chorus humming like a freshly tuned Lexus in a tasteful production. As well-written as this song is ("In the chill and sullen gray of morning, we play the parts that we have learned too well"), it could have become maudlin or self-pitying if less restraint and tact had been employed.

A mournful yet subdued clarinet, accompanied by Glen Hardin's subtle piano and James Burton's majestic, slightly foreboding guitar chords, eases us into the couple's bedroom as Elvis intones, "Lying by your side, I watch you sleeping," like a eulogy. Strings and orchestra come up, the lulling sound of occasional traffic, soothing the reflective lover. "I've lost you, though you're near me, and your body still is kind," Elvis laments, his voice moving as lushly as shifting satin sheets.

The "I've Lost You . . . reason can't stand in for feeling" refrain is bolstered by Ronnie Tutt's drums and cymbals. Various combinations of strings, tambourine, clarinet, and the Sweet Inspirations color but never obscure this simple yet unsolvable dilemma ("Softly, without pain, the joy is over"). A cello sighs deeply in the background. This is a mature, moving exposé of why people can sometimes no longer "talk it over," performed with professionalism and grace. Listen to how Elvis's voice communicates the achingly sad words "Six o'clock, the baby will be risin'." This recalls so tellingly the second line, "In your face the sweetness of a child."

Don't play this song if you're going through a breakup. On second thought, put it on right now.

♦ ♦ ♦ ♦

It was August 1970, and MGM was filming rehearsal footage, five different concerts from Las Vegas, and an opening in Phoenix for a musical documentary that had first been titled *Elvis's Summer Festival* and later was renamed *Elvis: That's the Way It Is*.

Following the month-long engagement in Las Vegas, Elvis planned to set out on his first substantial tour since the 1950s. He was

ecstatic about this and would often imagine all of the people coming to the auditoriums to see him perform, according to his bodyguards.

In his personal life, Elvis rarely went for one-night stands; he usually wanted to get to know his companions better. In August 1970, he met a woman with whom he would have one of his most lascivious, though brief, affairs.

Joe Esposito delineates the relationship in his book, *Good Rockin' Tonight*. The little-known actress's name was Barbara Leigh, and she was accompanied to one of Elvis's concerts by the head of MGM pictures, Jim Aubrey. At the time, Aubrey, along with Warren Beatty, Omar Sharif and Elvis Presley, was considered one of the most lustful lovers in Hollywood. In fact, Jackie Collins' book *The Stud* was taken from the libidinous adventures of Mr. Aubrey, who dated Barbara Leigh. Some even said they were engaged. Barbara was so attracted to Elvis Presley that she couldn't control herself. Although she professed her love for Aubrey, she was determined to have sex with Elvis, who was so enamored of Barbara that he couldn't resist her, either. The two spent a scintillating first night together, which was followed by more and more sexual encounters.

Esposito wrote that for many years Elvis had one steady woman, Priscilla, but there were also several others from around the country who would fly in to spend a week or so with the King whenever he beckoned. While these women were away from him, they were not to have sex with any other man. Most of them followed Elvis's dictum, but one who didn't was Barbara Leigh.

When Elvis learned that Leigh was involved in a tryst with Steve McQueen, while the two co-starred in the film *Junior Bonner*, he ended his sexual relationship with her. Leigh tried to mend things with Elvis, but through it all insisted that she was in love with Jim Aubrey. In the end, although Barbara and Elvis read spirituals together, they no longer had sex. Apparently, Elvis had lost all respect for her. For the rich and famous, the battle lines between the sexes are often twisted beyond belief.

It must be remembered that at the time of the Barbara Leigh affair, Elvis and Priscilla had been married for three years and were the parents of a baby girl. The King's lack of respect for their marriage was juvenile and disturbing.

Later, according to inside sources, Elvis would have a three-month affair with actress Cybil Shepherd. According to one of the King's friends, this was one of the least-gratifying relationships Elvis ever had, and Presley found ways, such as flaunting his drug-taking, to force Ms. Shepherd out.

♦ ♦ ♦ ♦

Bridge Over Troubled Water (*Walk a Mile in My Shoes* '70s boxed set, 1995)

This is one of the most-recorded songs in the history of music, and many critics believe that Elvis performed the finest versions, getting more out of the song than the composers ever intended. Of course, fans of Simon and Garfunkel might disagree.

J. D. Considine of *Rolling Stone* said this about the original Simon and Garfunkel smash hit: "Garfunkel's angelic tenor contrasted against the gospel piano." It was a stunning effort, bridging the chasm between late '60s cultural optimism and early '70s disillusionment.

The best studio version of this song that Elvis ever recorded appears on the *Walk a Mile in My Shoes* boxed set. Elvis gravitated toward "Troubled Water" like a pilgrim traveling to Mecca, and it was a linchpin for his early '70s live concerts. The live forays convinced the critics that Elvis performed this song the best, but there is a studio version that equals the live renditions.

In the *Walk a Mile* boxed set, listen to the soft violins and the warm percussion bells as Elvis sings, "When you're down and out, when you're on the street." Elvis pulls out all the stops, soothing, calming, revitalizing not just one generation but two, spanning the 1950s, '60s, and '70s. This "Troubled Water" stands as testimony to the King's enduring ability to put a smile on our faces, to make this world a little easier on our souls. "All your dreams are on their way" is a benediction in an incense-filled church. "I will ease your mind" caresses the high notes like lingering smoke. The high, sensitive yet steadfast notes are also essential because they convey Elvis's message that he is not only a friend one can rely on but a friend of strength and courage.

Elvis excels in this song because it allows him to elaborate on two of his most important values: friendship and loyalty ("see how they shine"). He conveys with conviction and confidence the belief that his friends will always have someone there to help carry the load.

Elvis's excellence in the higher vocal ranges is key to his performance of "Bridge Over Troubled Water," recalling the ghostly tenor on "Blue Moon" from the Sun sessions. Ironically, it was Elvis who made high notes less relevant to rock 'n' roll. He focused on feel and rhythm as the genre's most important aspects—which is also why Bruce Springsteen and Mick Jagger are superior to Pat Boone and Bobby Darin as rock singers.

You've Lost that Lovin' Feelin' (*Elvis: That's the Way It Is*, 1970)

With the exception of Elvis Presley and Bill Medley, no one sings this difficult song with any authority. In the many other versions, the guts are lost; there's no soul or power. Bill Medley was not a great singer, but his vocal gifts were well-matched to this song in the rarest of ways. Phil Spector produced a smash with "You've Lost that Lovin' Feelin'" by creating a record that could move mountains. The Righteous Brothers' version of this song is far better produced than are Elvis's renditions, but when it comes to singing, the King doesn't take a back seat to Bill Medley.

Elvis's best version of "You've Lost that Lovin' Feelin'" can be found on the *That's the Way It Is* documentary video. The version on the *That's the Way It Is* album is different and not quite as good, while the version recorded during the Madison Square Garden concerts is sung too fast.

On the documentary version, Elvis belts out the title verse like a Baptist preacher trying to cast out the devil. "Now it's gone, gone, gone, whoa whoa whoa" simmers as Elvis sings, lamenting, wondering, never vindictive or accusatory, only summoning the courage to tell it like it is, to plead with dignity for things to change. Ronnie Tutt's drumming is noteworthy, as he plays the full kit when needed ("something beautiful's dying") but exercises gentle restraint when the mood softens ("There's no tenderness in your fingertips"), in perfect synch with Elvis's shifting tempo and articulation.

Two memorable moments occur in this song. The first is when Elvis falters and begins the second verse, "There's no tenderness," with the first two words of the initial verse, "You never close your eyes." It's like he's been hit with a left hook but recovers immediately, achingly rendering "I reach out for you oo oo." For an instant he is truly lost, thus pulling the audience in, allowing us to identify with him, because we've all been there.

The second moment steals the show as Elvis crouches halfway down and sings, "Baby, baby, I get down on my knees for you." It's a movement that says: I'll do my part, sweetheart, but you gotta do yours ("If you would only love me, like you used to dooo, yeah"). The Sweet Inspirations nurture everybody, whispering "that's how much I love you" like leaves rustling in the wind, encouraging the lover's plea.

Elvis straddles the stage like a rodeo cowboy at the end ("And I can't go on whoaa, whoaa"), the tenuous vocals contradicting the pure physical presence, right arm back and punching out on a wild, emotional ride. Yet the words are questioning, still trying to revive a relationship waiting in Suite 707 of the International—or somewhere.

♦ ♦ ♦ ♦

Steve Binder once said that Elvis Presley was a man of "substance," was "street smart," and had a terrific "gut reaction." John Wilson, assistant director of *That's the Way It Is*, claimed that "Elvis had a great wit, personality, and intelligence." Bob Abel, director of the documentary *Elvis on Tour*, intoned that there was an "ingenius quality about Elvis."

All three were surprised that the King was much deeper than they had believed and was nothing like the shallow good ol' boy he portrayed in his movies. As the 1970s progressed, however, drugs dulled Elvis's mind and enthusiasm like a voodoo curse. Even on stage throughout most of the decade, his quick intellect and sharp sense of humor were replaced by incoherence and lame jokes. The King became a dullard before our very eyes.

During his peak years, however, Elvis displayed natural leadership qualities. Many who knew him believe that he could have been a riveting political or religious leader. He knew the walk, the talk, and how to keep people off balance while maintaining their adoration of him.

In the plethora of books written about Elvis by people who knew him, there is little insight into the man himself. A key reason for this, one that has never been exposed previously, is that Elvis Presley was never the same person to any two people he knew. Like Richard Nixon and Muhammad Ali, the King was a complex human being.

Jerry Schilling, the only person close to Elvis who really knew him, comments on what a nice guy he was. Regarding the King's intelligence, Schilling says, "Elvis was so sensitive, so quick, and so deep that I really feel like he had to go to the movies, and the amusement park, just to get things off his mind. They might seem like childish things for an adult to do, but it was a way of release." He also notes that "Elvis was so quick and sensitive he could walk into a room of 500 and know if you had a problem. He'd pull you to the side and say, 'Let's talk about it.' "

Bodyguard Dave Hebler put it this way in *Elvis: What Happened*:

> I have never seen before or since, never read of, never heard of, any man who so totally could disarm you with charm, generosity and what appeared to be spontaneous love, as could Elvis Presley. Today, you'd use the word *charisma*. Well, Presley had it to spare in truck loads. He could walk into a room, and without saying a word, fill it with sunshine. I later learned he could walk into the same room and fill it with black violence that could be very hard on the nerves. He could manipulate your emotions like no other human being on a series of highs and lows, dependent on his highs and lows.

When Elvis saw *Elvis: That's the Way It Is*, he was so excited that he watched it about a dozen times over the course of the next two weeks, people at MGM told us. Encouragingly, he was still in good shape for the November 1970 tour, but at times he seemed to be overwhelmed by the massive success of his comeback.

Less than a month after the November tour, Elvis had become bored with and disheartened by most of the things in his personal life and career. Perhaps no other performer has plunged from the heights of success to the depths of despair as quickly as Elvis Presley did. It is quite apparent that Elvis's deterioration began well before Priscilla left him, and that his behavior helped prompt her departure. Contrary to what many people believe, there were multiple factors besides his physical overindulgences that led to the King's Aristotlean fall from grace and majesty.

Elvis never got to do the overseas tour he so yearned for because Colonel Tom Parker kept postponing it. Although there has been much speculation about why he did so, the real reason was that the Colonel couldn't afford to leave the country and have his passport checked. You see, according to court documents, Tom Parker was not legally a citizen of the United States, and as had been known for some time, he was not a real colonel, either.

Mary in the Morning *(Elvis: That's the Way It Is, 1970)*

This song is pure unmitigated schlock and should never have been written or recorded. "I want to take her in my arms . . . the ache is there" is certainly not reciprocal affection because the girl is still asleep, "chasing the rainbow in her dreams." This is as cloying as Steve Lawrence's "Portrait of My Love," another song that drains all lifeblood and personality from the woman like a vampire. When Mary does awaken ("she turns to touch me"), she belongs to Dracula!

"Mary in the Morning" appears on the overrated *That's the Way It Is* album, and the sound quality here is as mushy as this song. It is Elvis's fault for having chosen this triviality, although he does try to make it work. The ensemble instrumentation is as competent as can be expected. Big deal. The basic problem is that even a little girl would ask daddy to sing a different song. Maybe something from *Mary Poppins*.

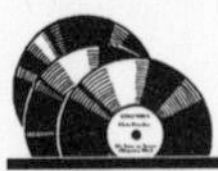

Walk a Mile in My Shoes (*Walk a Mile in My Shoes* '70s boxed set, 1970)

Although many are aware of the protest songs Elvis performed in the 1950s (in addition to 1968's "If I Can Dream" and 1969's "In the Ghetto"), few are familiar with the other socially conscious songs he did in the late '60s and in 1970. These include "Big Boss Man," "Long Black Limousine," "Change of Habit," "Clean Up Your Own Backyard," and "Walk a Mile in My Shoes."

Before singing "Walk a Mile" on stage, Elvis would tell the audience, "There was a guy who said one time, 'You never stood in that man's shoes or saw things through his eyes, or stood and watched with helpless hands while the heart inside you dies. So help your brother along the way, no matter where he starts—for the same God who made you made him too—these men with broken hearts.' " He spoke these words with sensitivity and sang the song with conviction.

"Walk a Mile" includes gospel-style interplay with the strong female chorus and moves with a cadence reminiscent of "Hey Jude." Elvis does not reach the Beatles' incredible crescendo here, but he allows the song to conclude prematurely, almost as if he knows that the audience's eruption that will follow will finish it for him.

Elvis Presley never got actively involved in politics, but two of his favorite leaders were Franklin Delano Roosevelt and John F. Kennedy. In the 1950s, Elvis was a social radical who wanted liberal change. In the late 1960s, Elvis was a social liberal. Steve Binder told us that the words to "If I Can Dream" reflected exactly what Elvis felt at the time. He was a staunch believer in the equality of mankind. In the 1970s, however, when hard drugs clouded his mind, Elvis moved to the right on the Vietnam war and the Communist threat. Too many critics pay undue attention to those distorted '70s—not that politics should matter when judging the artist.

Ice T's "Cop Killer," for example, is certainly not politically comparable to the Beatles' "Let It Be." Whether one agrees with the songs' messages or not, they are incisive works of art, drawing attention to injustice in different ways.

Snowbird (*Elvis Country*, 1971)

This is a contagious rendition of the Anne Murray hit. A bittersweet love song, it is sung effortlessly by Elvis, the tender words "so little snowbird take me with you when you go" crooned soft as the "gentle breezes" and "peaceful waters" he imagines. There's a sense of melancholy mingled with hope in the lines "The one I love forever is untrue, and if I could, you know that I would fly away with you." Elvis is excellent in this kind of setting ("Early Morning Rain" and "Always On My Mind," for example). Here, he draws the listener onto his patio, where he lounges alone on a hammock, reminiscing, singing aloud to the snowbird silhouetted by the "snowy mountain, cold and clean."

"Spread your tiny wings and fly away," backed by strings that are lush but not too strong, is delivered with a broken heart and a slight smile, perhaps addressed to a beautiful woman he is not yet ready for. Elvis is so comfortable singing "Snowbird" because it features his best vocal register, a beautiful baritone.

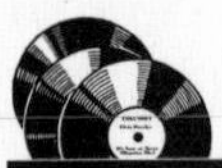

Whole Lotta Shakin' (*Elvis Country*, 1971)

Elvis sings the first three quarters of "Shakin' " in a roughshod manner, slurring the words in a muffled voice, as if experimenting during rehearsal. Potentially, he could have done a good job covering Jerry Lee Lewis's landmark rock 'n' roll statement, which was definitely among the best songs of the '50s—or ever. However, the Killer shoots the King down at high noon. Goodness, gracious—no contest.

Elvis does try to spur it up toward the end but is trampled by Jerry Lee's shakin' and bakin', slammin' and jammin', Michael Jordan at the piano. Elvis is supported by crisp drumming and a soaring, rebounding guitar, but the rally is too late and too little. The Killer owns this song, at home or on the road. We ain't fakin'!

This Is Our Dance (*Loveletters*, 1971)

We can hear rock 'n' roll lovers everywhere: What—are these guys crazy? (Maybe.) Why include this insipid, wedding-reception bullshit, Engelbert Humperdinck-type clinker in a survey of Elvis's music? Yeah, this is *The Last Waltz*, all right—not the Band and Dylan's fine concert and Scorsese's great film, but the Hump's big hit. It's Ed Ames's "My Cup Runneth Over," Barry Manilow's "Can't Smile Without You," Paul McCartney's "My Love." Are those strings Montovani or Percy Faith?

We chose to review this song because Elvis effortlessly fits into this standard's groove, further proving his diversity. Although we joke about this song, some older Elvis fans love it as one of their favorites.

Be honest. Didn't you dance real slow at the after-prom party to mediocre local band versions of Bread's syrupy "Make It With You" or Humperdinck's "Release Me"? (One day you threw your radio out the window when one of these tunes came on, but after a few cocktails, or whatever, you held your honey tight.) Face it—we all have sweet spots in our hearts for Hershey's Kisses ballads. "And when I hear you whisper 'You're mine,' we'll play that song just one more time," Elvis croons. "Ba ba ba ba boo," Bing Crosby chimes in with Elvis and the Lennon Sisters on *The Lawrence Welk Show*. There's a videotape somewhere, although we have no proof that it exists.

No, "Our Dance" can't match the Drifters' reflective "Save the Last Dance for Me," which reveals apprehension so skillfully, yet twirls around the ballroom, the swirling strings of the orchestra both soothing and menacing. "Our dance can last forever, and nobody knows what tomorrow will bring," Elvis seduces, without fear, and the strings wash away everything, a lover's voice.

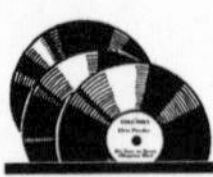

I Really Don't Want to Know *(Elvis: The Other Sides; Worldwide Gold Award Hits, Vol. 2, 1971)*

When Elvis begins, "Whoa, how many arms have held you and hated to let you go," he effectively draws out the diction, especially on "let," emphasizing the idea of not surrendering her, despite his conviction that she has played around. Terry Stafford's "Suspicion" ("Keeps us apart, why torture me?") and Elvis's own "Suspicious Minds" ("I can't walk out, because I love you too much, baby") are products of the same blues motif: the inability to face the music. Eric Clapton's "Layla," Ray Charles's "Your Cheatin' Heart," and Janis Joplin's "Piece of My Heart," all similarly stress the slender thread between weakness and strength, despair and possibility, that each of us has experienced when we know all is lost but somehow can't believe it.

The accompaniment is superb, the female chorus rising slightly after Elvis sings, "How many, oh how many, I wonder," full of pain, as if he is thinking about her after dropping her off at a restaurant to meet a girlfriend for lunch. It doesn't seem that he is singing here; it's as if we have tuned into a virtual reality of romantic turmoil.

James Burton's guitar work is impeccable, mimicking, expanding upon Elvis's obsession. He creates a moaning sound in the intro to blend with Elvis's first "whoa"—hints of the storm. At the end, he imitates this groove, only more mournfully, as the wind now blows back and forth. Elvis, the magnanimous prosecutor, seeks shelter. "Don't confess, just let it remain your secret," he sings softly, the Cadillac windows rolled up tight, so no one can hear as he cruises around town for a couple of hours in the rain.

♦ ♦ ♦ ♦

Elvis's drug-taking continued to increase, as did his neglect of Priscilla. Finally, in August 1972, Priscilla confronted Elvis. She wanted a divorce. Priscilla was having an affair at the time with karate instructor Mike Stone but, of course, Elvis had been having affairs all along. Even so, he was devastated. No woman left the King! Elvis believed his wife was jilting him for a nobody. He was being rejected—and Priscilla was still the love of his life.

The feelings of abandonment and the jolt to his ego made Elvis literally climb the walls in pain, according to his bodyguards, who also wrote that his consumption of drugs increased yet again.

Priscilla's departure, spawned by his own narcissism and inability to be a loving husband, catapulted the King into chaos.

Help Me Make It Through the Night (*Elvis Now,* 1972)

This is one of the few songs on which Elvis tries but doesn't sing with enough emotion. It's unimaginable that any woman but a diehard would be aroused by Elvis's ennervating, flaccid delivery of "Come and lay down by my side, 'til the early mornin' light." He simply misses the mark on this fine country ballad, a genre he almost always masters (listen to "Gentle On My Mind" and "Faded Love," for example).

On "Make It," his lover is more likely to respond to Elvis's self-pitying reading of "Let the devil take tomorrow, 'cause tonight I need a friend" by whispering a few words of encouragement over the phone, then revealing that she has an early morning business appointment. She knows intuitively that he is in no danger and will be himself again when the sun comes up.

When Jerry Lee Lewis performed this song in concert, after surviving a brush with death during one of his many hospital stays, every word meant something, as emotion dripped from the Killer and the audience. That's not the case here.

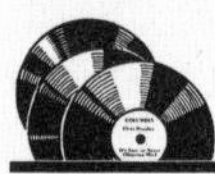

Hey Jude (*Elvis Now,* 1972)

Nobody has ever covered a Beatles song and improved on the original, so Elvis is in the company of many artists—distinguished to pedestrian—who have paid homage to the Fab Four with varying degrees of success. Jazz guitarist Wes Montgomery put a classy, personal stamp on "Day in the Life." Aerosmith does a passable "Come Together" but doesn't come close matching to the Beatles' jolting yet dreamy classic from *Abbey Road.*

Regrettably, Elvis's "Hey Jude" is only a notch above a Holiday Inn torch singer slithering through "Yesterday." His usually impeccable sense of pitch, timing, and phrasing hits an iceberg right at the start as he sings "don't be a fool" in the first line, instead of "don't make it bad," which is crucial to the song's meaning. Later, the Beatles' "making his world a little colder" is changed, mystifyingly, to "making his world a little better."

Elvis seems lost on this performance, and even laughs toward the end as the ship disappears beneath the waves, after the fourth of five contrived "Jude, Jude, ah Jude, Jude, ah Judy . . ." McCartney imitations. Elvis never gets into the song. The band needs a rescue boat, too: The horns are washed out; the strings and rhythm section struggle to remain afloat.

Fortunately, The Beatles idolized Elvis and never, as a group, dared to record any of his hits. Elvis should have returned the compliment.

Merry Christmas Baby *(Elvis Sings the Wonderful World of Christmas,* 1971)

This artful and sultry extended blues gem stands out on Elvis's Christmas album. It's the Paul Butterfield Blues Band's Chicago brand of hard blues, or early British Bluesbreakers style, stropped to a cutting edge. For all of Elvis's holiday sentimentality, Christmas seems to act as an aphrodisiac. First, it was "Santa Claus Is Back in Town" (1957) and now this.

Except for the relief of "Merry Christmas Baby," this 1971 compilation is one of the worst albums of Elvis's career, a lame Christmas album. The songs are lackluster, contrived traditional fare, and Elvis sings them listlessly, dispassionately. His 1957 record *Elvis's Christmas Album* is far superior, offering much creativity and inspiration.

"Merry Christmas Baby" doesn't even belong on the 1971 LP, because on this Yuletide surprise, Elvis oozes super-funky sensuality. He's having a ball, loose as can be. He got everything he wanted for Christmas, including "a diamond ring." What's he gonna give her? Himself, of course ("Well, I want to kiss you, baby, underneath your mistletoe"), a personalized X-rated movie!

Elvis sways and rolls, shuckin' and jivin' between verses, scattin' ("Mmmm," "Chop chop chop," "Yeahh!"), sometimes strange, indecipherable stuff, always riding the undulating swells and breaks of the superb supporting music. The piano alternately tinkles with excitement and swirls with pleasure, like sleigh bells. At one point, Elvis pushes even harder, yelling, "Wake up, Tutt!" at drummer Ronnie Tutt, then, "Dig in it, James" at brilliant lead guitarist James Burton, who has already completed a fireside solo. The excellent Charlie McCoy joins in the Christmas spirit on harmonica, creating a simmering tone just above the bass line, linking with the backbeat like a honey-baked ham coming out of the oven.

Anybody hungry? This is a Christmas feast for body and soul.

By early 1972, while Elvis was mainly interested in singing songs about his divorce, such as "Separate Ways" and "Always On My Mind," he was presented with an excellent rock 'n' roll song, "Burning Love." According to *Billboard*'s Phil Gelormine, Elvis recognized the song's potential but didn't want to record it. After considerable coaxing and pleading by Felton Jarvis and RCA, almost to the point of having to strap the King in a chair to force him to listen to the tune, Elvis agreed. During the initial run-through, Elvis got interested; in fact, he became psyched. He thought about how the song should be done and then proceeded to cut one of his greatest rock 'n' roll records.

Except for this song and a few others, another trend was developing: Elvis had let the 20- or 30-piece Joe Guercio ensemble essentially supplant his own band. This new orchestra diluted the sound of the superb James Burton-led 1969 band and did much harm to the lean, streamlined sinews of the music, although James Burton always shined. He was the essential player in Elvis's mind—the one man he could not go on stage without.

Elvis blundered when he allowed the Guercio orchestra to take over as his backup group. One of the reasons he did so was because, at this point in time, he did not fully appreciate the great music he had made in the past. Also, Elvis had always wanted to be accepted by a more sophisticated audience, but he failed to realize that his fans had grown less and less sophisticated, and that their knowledge of music had begun to wane as the '70s wore on. (The most likely explanation is that, as Elvis's concerts became worse, only the blindly loyal fans would show up for them.) Finally, the King's mind was so clouded by drugs that he actually thought Perry Como was making better music than the Rolling Stones!

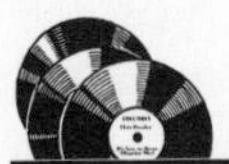

Burning Love *(Elvis's Greatest Hits,* 1981)

This is Elvis's purest rock 'n' roll song in years. James Burton propels the accompaniment with prolific guitar work and is supported superbly by Glen Harden on piano. Jerry Scheff's bass weaves and throbs with authority, and Ronnie Tutt's drums provide resonant, inventive cohesion. Elvis innovates with his vocal performance and inflections, flaming with a thrilling sexuality that he is continually overcome by. He delivers "Lord have mercy, I feel my temperature risin'" like a towering inferno, a crackling "hunka hunka burning love."

This may be Elvis's most exciting record. "Burning Love" attracted many young listeners to the King in the early '70s, listeners who previously had thought he was old-fashioned.

Elvis could play all rock 'n' roll instruments, and it is difficult to say which he played best. During the Sun sessions, although his rhythm guitar work was primitive, it nonetheless contributed to the invention of the modern rock format. Elvis's best rhythm guitar work can be found on "Reconsider Baby," where tightly strummed chords clash with vocals like crossed jumper cables.

The King would often joke that he only knew three chords, and until the Beatles, that's what rock 'n' roll was. Elvis was far from being a Keith Richards or Eric Clapton, but he never had to apologize for his musicianship.

Elvis's dynamism, grace, and instinct for dancing were essential to his ability to galvanize an audience. What we are referring to are his dance steps in the 1950s and in 1968, 1969, and 1970. During the 1960s, Elvis's movements in his movies were mediocre, and after 1970, he no longer performed his innovative freestyle dancing. All he did was shake. The more "into" a concert he was, the more he shook, a pale compromise when compared to what Elvis had done previously. Moreover, each year after 1969, his gyrations became fewer.

Elvis performed his last riveting choreography on stage in 1970. From 1971 through 1974, when he was "on," the King could still mesmerize an audience. During the final years of his life, however, his concerts became redundant and boring. Elvis Presley boring? Unfortunately, yes. Even on those nights when he made an effort (at the Uniondale, New York, show in 1975 and his 1976 Pittsburgh concert, for example), Elvis had lost the spark that could turn a single concert into an event of a lifetime. The magic was gone.

If you wish to see Elvis's greatest movements, watch the videos *This Is Elvis* and *Elvis: That's the Way It Is*. While they do not cover all of his stage techniques, they showcase many of the King's most powerful and distinctive moves. Although similar to *This Is Elvis*, *Elvis—The Greatest Performances, Vols. 1 and 2* are also worth viewing, especially the television special, *Elvis—The Greatest Performances*, hosted by Priscilla Presley. The two one-hour videos were combined into the two-hour TV presentation.

Michael Jackson is a better technical dancer; nobody was more intense in their prime than James Brown, while no one was more exciting than Jackie Wilson. Mick Jagger has a sense of ease, freedom and fervor, but it is probable that no one's movements were as innovative, dynamic, and electrifying as the King's. Elvis's charisma and sex appeal exploded like a pipe bomb in the groin of the audience. His '69 and '70 jumpsuits were wonderful stage wear and contributed more visual impact to the shows.

Upon seeing Elvis in concert, brilliant rock critic Jon Landau, current manager of Bruce Springsteen and Shania Twain, marveled: "There stood a man with more natural ability, talent and soul than I expect to see on the stage at any rock concert."

Could Elvis have become a great actor? That's a difficult question to answer. He was not the "natural" that Marlon Brando, Montgomery Clift, and James Dean were, but he showed promise in his early films, particularly *Jailhouse Rock* and *King Creole*, delivering convincing performances in both movies. A major flaw with Elvis was that he never took acting lessons, which are almost essential to becoming technically proficient. Many actors, including the outstanding Burt Lancaster, are strong when conveying feeling but weak when it comes to technique. Elvis Presley suffered from the same deficiency.

Nevertheless, his charismatic stage presence, combined with dedicated direction and better roles, could have made Elvis a better actor. It is unrealistic, however, to believe that he could have become a great one.

In 1972, the King and the Colonel agreed to do another music documentary, called *Elvis On Tour*. His performance was sloppy, slipshod, and hurried, while the film quality and direction were awful. During Elvis's most dramatic moments, the camera was focused on a flute player, the band, or some other distraction.

In 1972 Elvis was presented with another opportunity to prove he was the King of Entertainment: a January 1973 satellite broadcast from Hawaii that would be shown live on closed-circuit, and later on tape, to virtually the entire world. Most countries would receive the broadcast live, while the U.S. would get it on a delayed basis in April 1973. Facing such a challenge, Elvis markedly reduced his drug consumption, lost 25 pounds (he was not that heavy in 1972), and got himself into great shape, according to his bodyguards. The event would be called *Elvis: Aloha from Hawaii.*

The economic results were stunning—even for Elvis. Here are just a few of the numbers: in England, 90 percent of all closed-circuit locations sold out a month before the concert. Japan reported that *Aloha* posted that nation's highest television ratings ever. In the Philippines, E1 Salvador, and Thailand, the special attracted a staggering 91.8 percent of the viewing audience. Hong Kong reported that one million inhabitants watched the show, and Korea and other countries around the globe likewise reported huge TV audiences. When the special was broadcast in the United Stated in April, it was the week's number-one show and also ranked as one of the top-rated TV specials ever. A billion and a half people saw *Elvis: Aloha from Hawaii*, surpassing all later satellite concerts, such as Michael Jackson, Madonna, and Live-Aid, as well as the number of people who saw Neil Armstrong become the first man to walk on the moon.

Elvis's performance, however, was not a unanimous winner, and for the first time since his '68 *Comeback Special*, there were some negative reviews. Many thought he would rip into this concert and make it as memorable as the 1968 Burbank sessions or even the 1969 Las Vegas concerts. Instead, he delivered a middle-of-the-road performance. He hardly moved—that was deliberate—and some of the songs Elvis often danced to in his regular concerts weren't even included in his *Aloha* repertoire. There were few definitive versions of his songs in the special, and Elvis sang most of the play list straight, rarely utilizing gradations of color and tone, or tapping his wellspring of skills, or exhibiting much effort. Yet he made the show successful anyway.

Elvis was sending a message that his wild "Elvis the Pelvis" days were over, and he was now a middle-aged entertainer. The King looked and sounded great in this new persona, though, and had a trump card for this broadcast: He would sing most of the songs with understated beauty. That was why his older audience loved this special so much. Nevertheless, although both *The '68 Comeback Special* and *Aloha* are available on videotape, the *Comeback Special* has outsold *Aloha* by a margin of three to one, proving that rock 'n' roll lovers, casual fans, and the public prefer the King of Rock 'n' Roll over the King of Entertainment. Clearly, the highlight of *Aloha* is "American Trilogy."

A rehearsal show Elvis did at the same site is available on video and is recommended for insomniacs only. The camera isn't focused on Elvis at the dramatic, key moments here, either. The King donated his proceeds from the *Aloha* special to a Hawaiian cancer charity.

♦ ♦ ♦ ♦

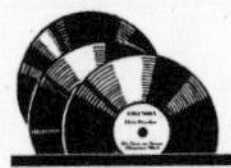

I'm So Lonesome I Could Cry (*Elvis: Aloha from Hawaii*, 1973)

This live rendition was one of the highlights of the 1973 *Aloha from Hawaii* satellite special. Elvis sings it as a straight country-western song, with the accent perhaps more than ever before on cowboy music. When he draws out the world "lonesome," there's the edge of a yodel.

Elvis allows the whole world to glimpse his soul for a couple of minutes, a year after his divorce from Priscilla, without all the glitz and glamor. The lonesome cowboy persona is perfect, and Elvis plays with the image. When he sings, "The silence of a falling star lights up a purple sky," he testifies to everyone that there is so much to say that he can't touch, can't share, but the "purple sky" reference reveals his unresolved passion, grief, redemption. "Did you ever see a robin weave, when leaves begin to die?" is a beautiful line and is perhaps sung with prescience of his own death and a heart full of soul as his voice warbles on the word "die."

The steely yet simpatico guitar supplements the country flavor of Elvis's journey, especially after the line "that means he's lost the will to live" and in the mournful intro to "Here alone, somewhere away."

Aloha. Book 'em, Dano.

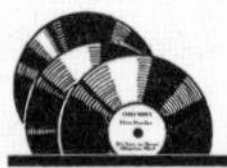

American Trilogy *(Elvis: Aloha from Hawaii, 1973)*

Mickey Newbury's "American Trilogy" is given a resounding, infectious treatment on 1973's *Aloha* special. The song is an artistic and incisive amalgamation of "Dixie," "The Battle Hymn of the Republic" and "All My Trials."

He digs into his Mississippi and Tennessee roots when he sings "for in Dixieland I was born . . . I'll take my stand," slouching leisurely at first, legs akimbo, leaning back as if on a porch swing in Tupelo, then standing tall for "Look away, look away," at once steadfast in his faith and chagrined regarding the South he loves so much. James Burton stands next to Elvis, guitar in hand like a wayward Rebel rifle, dressed in matching white, finally looking like the rock star he has every right to be.

Ronnie Tutt's drums signal "Battle Hymn" hard as a military salute, and Elvis belts out "Glory, glory hallelujah," his right hand flashing out across his chest (and later slashing like a whip), as he commands respect from the audience while the Sweet Inspirations live up to their name. "His truth is marching on" is delivered patriotically, as the chorus reaches higher, the strings kick in, and the muzzled horns steer us to another level of involvement.

The stirring words "so hush little baby . . . your daddy's bound to die" are pure gospel, homage to the ideal of sundering all barriers of race, creed, and color—and ending international strife (in 1973, the war in Vietnam finally ceased). This is Elvis's trilogy, clinging to dreams of the Old South yet challenging all the obstacles to true freedom at the same time.

The final "Glory, glory," after "all my trials will soon be over" and a gorgeous flute solo by a black session player, segues into a shot of Elvis staring across the stage, smiling and ready, half in a trance, sweat dripping off his face, barking out signals to the band like a four-star general in the heat of battle. Then, he abruptly barrels into "truth is marching on" again, with a whole new meaning, the "onnnn" needing no satellite transmission to get the point across.

According to the Memphis Mafia, the King was pleased with the way *Elvis: Aloha from Hawaii* turned out, but with the challenge gone, he again started gaining weight and strongly increasing his drug intake. Things became so bad that Elvis checked himself into a Memphis hospital in August 1973 in an attempt to overcome what was now controlling his life. It didn't work, and his downward spiral continued.

CHAPTER 7

The Seventies: Sunset in Las Vegas

There really is no appropriate way to introduce this final chapter of Elvis's life. Sunset, in Las Vegas, is when life begins. The gamblers hover around the blackjack and crap tables. The lights are bright and hearts are light, until kings over queens, or snake eyes destroy everything you ever believed was possible, until you bet more than you can afford to lose and throw the dice one last time in pursuit of immortality.

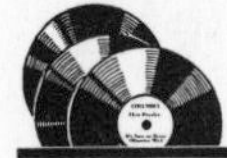

Find Out What's Happening *(Raised on Rock, 1973)*

When Elvis went into the Stax Studios in Memphis to record, he was surrounded by a mixture of his own players and other musicians, some who were in awe of him and others who laughed at his ridiculous song selections. *Raised on Rock* is the first "Priscilla album," a collection devoted mainly to lamenting the loss of the love of Elvis's life, Priscilla. According to sources at the studio, some of the Stax musicians wondered whether the guy with the sideburns was Elvis Presley or Engelbert Humperdinck. As a result, they lacked enthusiasm on these sessions, and that really dimmed Elvis's interest. The outcome was songs without direction, focus, or tension. "Find out what's happening"—about what?

This is the only time in Elvis's career that he is bored singing rock 'n' roll. "Before I say farewell, I'll give you just another day, you better find out . . ." comes across distracted, as if he couldn't care less who he's singing to or what is happening. The chorus is mixed way too low, especially on "Baby, you know it's true," the female vocalists rolling their eyes with their voices, waiting for this lame date to end. The organ behind "tell me what you're gonna do" is almost inaudible, like listening to a funeral from outside the church. The guitar and drums on the break, after "I'm gone now," are clueless. So are we.

♦ ♦ ♦ ♦

In the early 1970s, Elvis met the classy and sexy Linda Thompson. For a year, he was completely monogamous with her, and they had a fine relationship, Linda stated on a television program, and Elvis finally showed some maturity in a relationship with a woman. Nevertheless, his drug-taking continued—as did his pining for Priscilla. Although he would remain with Linda for a few more years, after the inital period of faithfulness, Elvis told her that he would not continue to be monogamous. Linda, who was truly in love with Elvis, accepted this arrangement and remained devoted to him.

Several of Elvis's friends, including Ed Parker, told us that the King was a changed man during this period. He was no longer fun-loving and lively, but could be brooding, violent, obsessed as any solipsistic dictator. He shot out TV sets and even pulled guns on his bodyguards, sometimes pointing them at their temples. He would take his entourage to mortuaries to study corpses and discuss embalming. This was the same person who nearly ruined Marty and Patsy Lacker's marriage. Almost like a strange cult leader, Elvis controlled Marty (as he did virtually all of the Memphis Mafia), and as a result, Patsy became secondary in Marty's life. Elvis was so fractured mentally that he thought he could perform faith healing. In spite of his rude or thoughtless behavior, he could talk his way out of anything.

Just as a child feels guilty after doing something wrong, Elvis exhibited so much sorrow and concern that nobody could stop loving him. His huge intake of drugs and the resultant crashing boredom led to all kinds of crazy thoughts and deeds. The King was falling from grace like Shakespeare's Lear, allowing demons to possess him.

Andy Klein of Beta Research, a contributing editor to Phil Gelormine's original *Elvis World,* related to us how Elvis, his band, and producer Felton Jarvis went into the studio to do an album in 1974. As they were getting things ready, Elvis was in the mood to do Chuck Berry's "Promised Land" for fun. The run-through went so well that Jarvis suggested they record the song. The King agreed and rendered a vivacious version of the rambling classic—improving on Berry's version by an impressive margin.

After that cut was completed, Elvis sang several paltry ballads that made the album quite ordinary. However, he was so out of touch that he actually thought the ballads were the important music—almost as if he had forgotten what he had just accomplished.

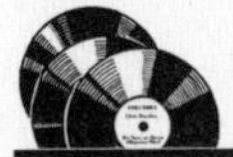

Promised Land (*Promised Land,* 1975)

Elvis gives a rousing, rambunctious, hell-bent-for-leather reading of this outstanding Chuck Berry composition, picking up on Berry's

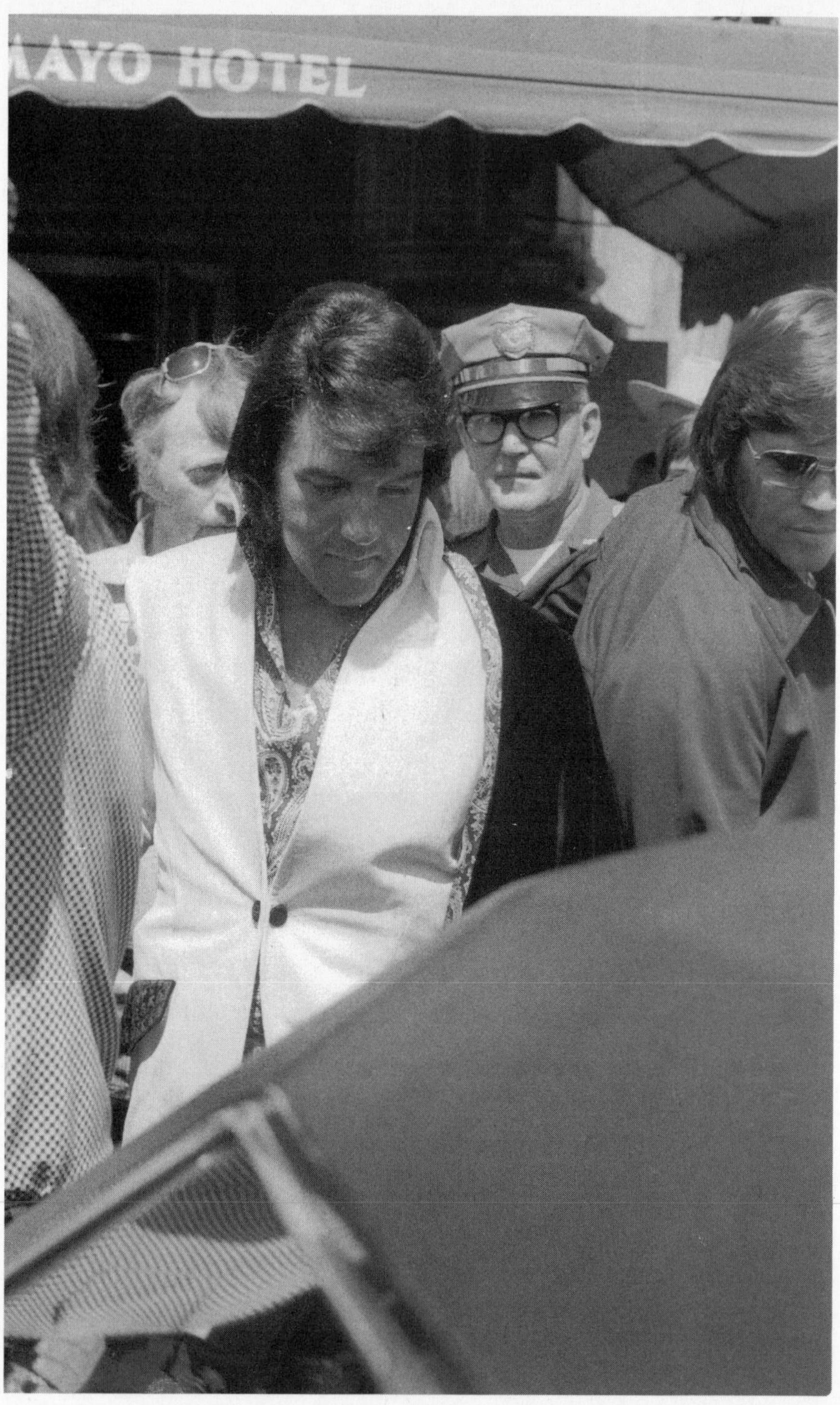
MAYO HOTEL

marvelous (as usual) sense of humor and absurdity. The King has a ball of a wild ride from Norfolk, Virginia, to New Orleans, and to Los Angeles by bus ("That Hound broke down and left us all stranded"); by the *Midnight Flyer* from Birmingham to Louisiana; then somehow heads to Houston, where "people . . . care a little about me." There's the twinkle of a prairie star in Elvis's voice as he catapults across rails and down highways, accelerating the cadences like the clack-clack-clack of train wheels or the whooshing of a vehicle speeding past telephone poles on the roadway at night.

Suddenly, he's "high over Albuquerque on a jet to the promised land." Maybe some rich oil folks in Houston helped him out. We all know he's going to make it OK. Elvis takes the good-ol'-country-boy timbre of this vocal to the max at the end when he arrives at LAX, crying out to the pilot, "cut your engines and cool your wings," one of Chuck Berry's best lines. After running to the telephone, he connects ("Tell the folks back home this is the promised land callin', and the poor boy's on the line"). This is a breakneck, devil-may-care odyssey of a young man with nothing to lose, all of life's mirages for now as real as a drive-in movie screen in a lonely desert town on Friday night.

Elvis's opening line, "Ah, get on it," is delivered with reckless abandon. James Burton's guitar churns like a locomotive throughout the song, keeping it on track, roaring through tunnels, rattling bridges over deep chasms. The bass and drums are as rhythmic as a chain gang on tornado watch, dancing with rakes and shovels. The piano's trills and glissandos hold on for dear life.

This is an enjoyable recording. Bruce Springsteen sang, "Yes, I believe in the promised land." So did Martin Luther King, and we listened. We also believe in this "Promised Land," just for the fun of it, just for the taste of hitting the road again without a care in the world.

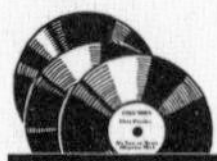

It's Midnight *(Promised Land,* 1975)

No, this song is not ground from the same grist as Eric Clapton's classic "After Midnight," when "we gonna let it all hang down." Hardly. Elvis sings as if the stroke of midnight has thrust him into an episode of *Tales from the Crypt*, into a bedroom full of heartache, ghosts, and horrifying apprehension ("needing you, wishing I could be the man I try to"), unable to deal with the loss of his woman. This is no hunka hunka burning love—Elvis is trapped in a raging backdraft and can only lament ("knowing you don't love me like you used to").

The cut from *Memories of Elvis* is better than the version on *Promised Land*, in which Elvis's vocal is drowned out by too much orchestral backup. On *Memories*, the engineering lessens the support, going basically with sweet country guitar (especially in the intro) and drums, quite effective when Elvis sings, "It's getting late, and I know that's when I am weak." The trouble is, they mixed Elvis's voice too high and strong, so that a bit of poignancy is lost sometimes. For instance, "And just forget you. Whoaaa, but it's midnight" should sound more tender. Yet the listener is treated in both of these musical readings to the gifts of a singer who often is better than his song.

The first edition of *Rolling Stone Rock Lists* comments that while *Blue Hawaii* wasn't a bad musical, it should have been the worst Elvis ever made. However, the King appeared in many more that made *Blue Hawaii* look as good as *Gigi*. "It's Midnight" should have been the worst ballad Elvis sang in the 1970s—it's an average song.

Yet sadly, by 1973, after he and Priscilla had separated and divorced, album after album featured begrudging, boring, repetetive "Priscilla ballads"—in which Elvis would mourn her departure and plead for her to come back to him. Most of these ballads are exasperating and cloying.

It surprises many critics when they learn that many diehard fans prefer the "Priscilla ballads" over any of his other music. The answer is very simple: This is the most personal Elvis has ever been, and he relates to these devotees with feelings of pain and desperation. These ballads represent a rare familial attachment between artist and audience.

♦ ♦ ♦ ♦

On September 27, 1974, in College Park, Maryland, Elvis again made history. It was the first concert at which he arrived so stoned on drugs that he couldn't perform. He fell to his knees as he stepped from his limousine, waving back the people who crowded around to help. Once on stage, he had to use the microphone stand to prop himself up. He was so drugged that he couldn't talk coherently, let alone sing, calling to mind Jim Morrison at the end.

Although Elvis managed to complete that tour, similar incidents occurred in Detroit and Indianapolis. He mumbled like a mummy through 14 songs and, when he spoke, used some of the worst language ever heard on stage, similar to early Iggy Pop or Johnny Rotten.

For the first time since his comeback, Elvis actually heard some boos from the crowd, but not from most of its members. The loyalists forgave him—convincing themselves that the star just wasn't feeling well. Much of the audience had too much respect for the King to dissent openly, but they were very disappointed.

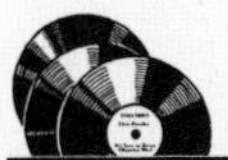

Honky Tonk Angel *(Promised Land, 1975)*

Elvis once said he probably knew every gospel song ever sung. If gospel is the foundation of his music, then country is the struts and studs. Randy, Garth, Billy Ray, Wynonna, Shania, and Dolly could hear "Honky Tonk Angel" today and pair off for a nice slow glide across a Nashville dance floor, cheek to cheek, jeans tucked into their boots. Elvis slips into the melancholy mood of this song like a battered Chevy S-10, feeling all the familiar bumps in the dirt road leading home ("But there's a honky tonk angel, who'll take me back in").

Many country songs portray volatile situations, a finger on the trigger, without the explosion (Dolly Parton's "Jolene" comes to mind). That's part of their beauty—it's all in the tension, up to the listener to resolve. "Honky Tonk Angel" fits this groove like Wynonna's black stockings. "When was the last time you kissed me?" Elvis issues softly at the beginning. The piano is languorous and beckoning.

In his late-'60s country/pop hit "Poor Side of Town," Johnny Rivers sang, "The last time I saw you, you wouldn't even kiss me," but Johnny didn't have an angel up his sleeve. Despite Elvis's advantage, we still feel his pain ("So tell me if you think it's over, and I'll leave it up to you how it ends"), but he can't help but revel a bit in his position of power. "Mmmm," he moans after the last chorus of "Honky tonk angel who will take me back in," full of sexual innuendo. Gentle strings at the end, as the chorus repeats, soften the sting she must feel.

Should we be on Elvis's side? Yeah, everybody has felt this kind of bitterness. But is his partner totally to blame? Has Elvis been with his angel since they've been together? Probably not. However, the lines "It's been a long time since you've felt like my woman—even longer since I felt like your man" reveal romantic/ sexual frustration that forces recollection. On "She's waiting, Lord, she's happy just holdin' my hand," "waiting" is squeezed by Elvis's voice like a pillow.

Meanwhile, Elvis's old flame is putting a remastered edition of

Rosie and the Originals' "Angel Baby" into the CD player of her new Firebird Formula.

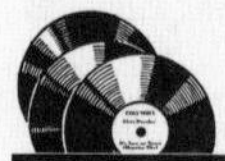

T-R-O-U-B-L-E (*Elvis Today*, 1975)

This Chuck Berry-inspired song ("Promised Land," "Johnny B Goode," and "Maybelline" come to mind) was written expressly for Elvis Presley by Jerry Chesnut, and it is perhaps the most underrated rocker of the King's career. Ronnie Tutt's drums thump the floor like beer kegs being unloaded from a truck at a honky-tonk; James Burton's guitar keeps the funky stage lights blinking; Glen Harden's piano lines get a thousand toes movin' in their boots; and the whole mix recaptures the great echo sound of Elvis's 1950s recordings. There are times when his rapid-fire vocals almost blow out the mike, trying to cram every bit of information into the record like a test pilot whose plane is shaking.

"T-R-O-U-B-L-E" combines the roots of early rock 'n' roll with the technology of the day. The lyrics are about a piano player in a lounge who one night sees a girl come in who is so good-looking that she startles him. The lyrics are simple, but Elvis sings them eagerly. He's enraptured by what he sees, thinking about her and wondering why she's alone, surmising that "her mother must have been a good-looking mother too." He believes that someone so good-looking has to be T-R-O-U-B-L-E.

Elvis exhibits increased stimulation ("told me not to stare because it was impolite, and did the best she could to try to raise me right, hey, but mama never told me nothin' about somethin' like Y-O-U") and lustfulness ("lookin' like glory and walkin' like a dream").

Here, Elvis gives the listener a picture of danger spiked with potential compliance, again demonstrating that he has never lost touch with his working-class roots. He is not the "King," who can have any woman; he is the piano player, who can only watch and observe from a distance. This is no high-class lounge, and he is not longing for a socialite. Indeed, she might wear enough makeup for a Van Gogh painting, her racy dress creating hot static, picking up cigarette ashes as she sashays by the ramshackle tables. The killer lines are "Well, you talk about a troublemaker . . . the men are gonna love and all the women gonna hate, remindin' them of everything they never gonna be—maybe the beginning of World War III!"

"T-R-O-U-B-L-E" has been recorded by country singer Travis Tritt, and while he performs the song adequately, he lacks the rock and blues influences that give the song some of its spice. Elvis also injects the right touch of humor.

♦ ♦ ♦ ♦

As Elvis's behavior became more and more bizarre, people began to wonder. On some of his tours, the King would take along his latest girlfriend, while Linda Thompson accompanied the entourage, acting like Elvis's sister and nurse. Yet nobody said a word. Muhammad Ali used to do the same thing. Elvis was at such a point of decline that he didn't see anything strange about this scenario.

My Way (*Walk a Mile in My Shoes* '70s boxed set, 1995)

No one, including Elvis Presley, has ever come close to singing "My Way" as well as Frank Sinatra did. Paul Anka wrote the song for Frank, whose matchless phrasing, like a word sculpture, carved the song into an eternal masterpiece. Yet Elvis makes "My Way" work because the song requires musical stature and public recognition that few possess. His best version is on the *Walk a Mile in My Shoes* '70s boxed set. On the live renditions, however, Elvis's phrasings are sloppy as he sings too fast—sometimes words are only half-pronounced—and the performances are slipshod.

On the *Walk a Mile* studio version of "My Way," however, his delivery is introspective and sensitive, sung as if Elvis is telling a small group of friends about "each charted course, each careful step along the byway." When he sings, "I faced it all, and I stood tall," his voice breaks slightly on the second "I" but gathers strength again for the words "and did it my way." The accompanying piano and chorus never intrude on Elvis's vocals but provide respectful encouragement, which the King does seem to need. He is much more somber and restrained than Sinatra, who is full of dash and vinegar when he renders: "The record shows, I took the blows and did it my way," despite recognizing his flaws.

The King's "My Way" can't touch the Chairman of the Board's, but Elvis clearly produces an intimate interpretation—his way.

The bodyguards and others painfully recount that Elvis's drug-taking had reached such an alarming level that he overdosed three times (Linda Thompson was there to save him) before he accidentally killed himself. Ginger Alden, Elvis's new steady, was on hand when Elvis died. She tried to help, but it was too late.

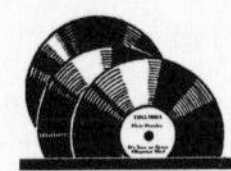

Always On My Mind (*Separate Ways* [Camden], 1976; you may have to accept an abbreviated *This Is Elvis* soundtrack, 1981)

This love song was made famous by Willie Nelson, but Elvis actually recorded it first. Although there is too much orchestration in the production (the piano and steel guitar would have been fine by themselves without the cello and the orchestral and choral support), Elvis overcomes this conceptual deficiency. He modulates the enunciation of words and phrases to evoke a range of emotions: lamentation and lassitude, yearning and hope. In the line "little things I should have said and done, I just never took the time," he stretches out the sorrow, pulsing like a digital clock, wishing he could have her back, cutting to the heart. "Give me give me one more chance to keep you satisfied," Elvis pleads, but without sentimentality, his voice rising plaintively at the end of "satisfied."

When recording this song, which is featured in the movie *This Is Elvis*, the King would turn away from the microphone and grimace because the pain was too much to bear.

Still, "Always On My Mind" remains the signature of the country "Outlaw," Willie Nelson.

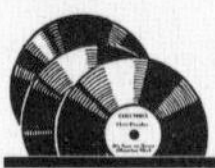

Pieces of My Life (*Elvis Today,* 1975)

A hidden autobiography, this is Elvis's life as he sees it fragmenting during his final years, sung with a thousand lifetimes' worth of experience. The phrase "and you know who" refers to Priscilla and reveals caverns of self-doubt and blame. The song proffers such sadness and pitch-black despondency, it's enough to "make a grown man cry," the naked boulevard of his soul. The band respectfully plays as softly as a funeral dirge, and Elvis sings with such emotion that it sounds as if he's coming apart—which he is.

The evocation brings to mind the words of *Billboard*'s Phil Gelormine when he wrote, "Elvis had no skin, he was all raw nerves and it was the secret of his musical genius." Roberta Flack sang "Killing Me Softly with His Song" (1973), which now sounds like a foreshadowing of Elvis's decline.

At the end, Elvis Presley was so warped by drugs that he couldn't control his bodily functions and had to wear diapers, which he couldn't even change on his own. Why did he tumble so rapidly? Why did the King of Hearts deal himself out of the game of life before our very eyes? Elvis constantly needed new challenges and sensations. When he was no longer satisfied nor tested, when indifference submerged the thrills, boredom's tentacles drowned him. Lack of discipline, self-indulgence, too little maturity, absence of direction—all fed his artificial appetite.

"How do you save a man from himself?" Dave Hebler asked at a press conference shortly after the King's death. Surely, the doctors should be held responsible for prescribing so many pills, but it is equally true that Elvis would have gotten the drugs from someone else, if he had to. Roadies and toadies and Hollywood moguls and madames of the night either tried to help or felt helpless, or nudged him over the edge. Maybe we ourselves are at fault for expecting so much from the beginning.

Many people and things can be blamed for his demise, but the real cause of Elvis Presley's destruction was the man himself.

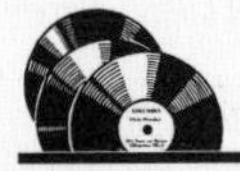

Hurt *(From Elvis Presley Boulevard, Memphis, Tennessee,* 1976)

Phil Gelormine wrote that when Elvis sang "Hurt," it "wasn't a song but a cry for help." The King turns in one of his most harrowing performances here, a two-minute, ten-second attempt to let out all the unrelieved agony he feels, crying out for a reprieve from his pain. When he laments, "way down deep inside of me," he takes every lost lover there. In the phrase "never, ever part," the word "never" is drawn out as though it truly means "eternity." Elvis's voice shakes with the words "breaks my heart."

When he pours out "even though you hurt me like nobody else could ever do," his voice begins with a soft growl and builds with such fragility that he convinces us that he never thought betrayal was possible. Instead of revenge, he wants only to unburden himself of what he feels. The spoken middle section, ending with "because I still love you so," defines helpless seductiveness. The final syllable is a piercing, shivering note of vocal power and emotional torment, as Elvis achieves a temporary catharsis.

For the Heart *(From Elvis Presley Boulevard, Memphis, Tennessee, 1976)*

Elvis has the necessary energy on this rocker but doesn't sing with a rock 'n' roll voice; his uptempo country delivery lacks sufficient grit and grind. The band, especially Glen D. Hardin's cookin' keyboards and Ronnie Tutt's drums, supplies a solid bottom line, and James Burton punches out rhythmic lead-guitar licks, although they are somewhat drowned out in the mix. The biggest problem is the Stamps Quartet, especially J. D. Sumner, who just drag the song down.

Due to the shortcomings of Elvis, Sumner, and the Stamps, what could have been a fine song motors across the finish line near the end of the pack. The pit crew (Hardin, Tutt, Burton) does its best but can't make up precious seconds lost to the driver's poor concept, focus, and fortitude.

By this time Elvis was as burned out with women as he was with his career. There were many times when he would spend the night with a woman but not have sex with her. Most of these women complained to members of the Memphis Mafia, for it was their intent to "make it" with the King, as Elvis's stepbrothers, the Stanleys, note in their book, *Love Me Tender*. "Love Me Tender"—isn't that a love song?

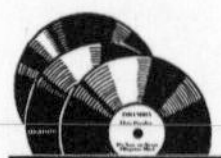

Moody Blue *(Moody Blue, 1977)*

Elvis never performed disco, but this is as close as he ever came. Andy Klein jokes that "Moody Blue" is the "best disco song ever recorded."

Elvis's feel for the music is clear, and he captures the bewilderment, bemusement, and confusion of the song, while at the same time exuding unmistakable charm. The band does more than just support Elvis; in fact, the backup players play a significant role in giving the song its bounce and beat.

This is not a great rocker by any means, but it's an enjoyable record if you're in the mood. Recorded during the era of the Bee Gees' "Stayin' Alive" and Donna Summer's "Hot Stuff," "Moody Blue"—although not intended to be rock/disco—scored high on the dance charts.

♦ ♦ ♦ ♦

Elvis had grown very tired of Linda Thompson, a woman who had proven to be a devoted companion. Elvis did love Linda, so he couldn't bring himself to ask her to leave. Instead, he spent little time with her and was always with other women. Finally, Linda got the message and left. Essentially, Elvis drove her away: still cheating on her, still searching for the key to love's door.

The King's next steady was a young beauty queen, Ginger Alden, a very attractive, spunky, saucy woman who would stand up to him. Elvis was envigorated by this change of recipe, even though the Memphis Mafia, as they stated to us, didn't like her because of her independence. Practically everyone close to Elvis that we talked with confirmed this.

Ginger was Elvis's last hope. He lost considerable weight, whipped himself into pretty good shape, and, in the final days of 1976, put on the best concerts he had performed since Uniondale, New York, in 1975. The Uniondale concert had also been prompted by a fling with a woman, the blonde Diane Goodman.

Within months, however, the excitement and challenge provided by Ginger lost its spice. Elvis's drug-taking increased dramatically, and he looked and acted as if he might not survive the next minute.

♦ ♦ ♦ ♦

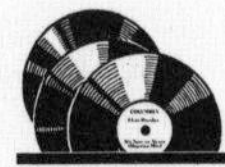

Little Darlin' *(Moody Blue,* 1977)

This is a concert song done as a joke; nonetheless, much more comes through. Elvis recreates the '50s feel, a genie's response to a wish.

Maurice Williams and the Gladiolas' original is the best version. The Diamonds' huge hit plays more heavily on the song's inherent youthful, bashful humor (legend has it that they were a struggling jazz/vocal band that recorded it as a lark). Elvis deliberately camps it up here, affectionately mocking the period he epitomized. He comes across like one of the boys in the gym, zapping other boys with wet towels, acting out how he is going to ask the blonde head cheerleader for a date, then collapsing in laughter. Elvis hits the final high note like a teenage girl. He's having a ball. Isn't that what it's all about?

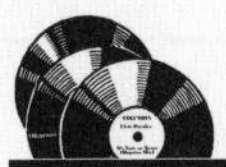

Way Down *(Moody Blue,* 1977)

A poorly written rock song, "Way Down" is full of superficial sensuality. Elvis seems listless, even careless at times with his vocals, rushing through lines, blurring pronunciations. The backup chorus, especially J. D. Sumner's bass voice, seems to duel with the band to see which can grab more attention. Sumner's final "way on down" is so overdone that it sounds like a caricature of "Old Man River." For Elvis to give Sumner—a weak, downer of a singer—this much time on a record proves that he lost all of his capacity to make great records.

Recorded in 1976, "Way Down" is a good example of the King's frequent inability to make sound musical judgements during his final years. Chubby Checker sang, "How low can you go." Elvis is stuck in rock limbo.

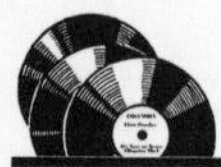

She Thinks I Still Care *(Moody Blue, 1977)*

This country-flavored effort is one of the better "Priscilla ballads." Here Elvis sings with more sincerity than sentimentality, drama replacing melodrama. It's not a song that is deep in the poetry department, but the King employs his trademark gift to elevate the lines to a higher plane. At points, he seems to sing in blocks of time, or as though his voice is gradually climbing. This elongated syncopation is almost a symphonic cadence.

Elvis wrings real pathos from "just because, Lord, I saw her and went to pieces." The strings signal the final reprise, eloquently, thoughtfully, as if trying to convince the bereft singer that the walls are not closing in, yet betraying to the listener that he is all too aware of what has been lost.

The voice undulates between bitterness and sorrow. "Well, if that silly notion brings her cheer" is sharp vinaigrette with more than a touch of sugar, while "just because I haunt the same old places" (with the female chorus echoing "same old places" beautifully, as if Elvis is in a cave) hints at the edges of despair ("the memory . . . lingered everywhere").

Then come the silvery yet rough tones ("Tell me where did she get, Lord, such an idea, yeah, oh oh," which soften into personal insight ("just because I asked a friend about her") as the female chorus sings "oooooooo."

James Burton's alternately bass and treble blues/country guitar, low at first on "Oh, just because I spoke her name somewhere," becomes soft as a mountain stream on the middle refrain ("She still thinks I care"), enhancing Elvis's fluctuating moods.

All former lovers, regardless of who they are with, cannot help but shuffle on the couch when they hear this song—and then hold on for dear life.

♦ ♦ ♦ ♦

The last eight months of Elvis's life were spent taking a pharmacopoeia of drugs that actually distorted his face and body, sapped his vital organs, and engorged his heart. The King was almost entirely bedridden during those final months. Shortly before Elvis's death, former bodyguards Red West, Sonny West, and Dave Hebler, who had been fired by the King, came out with the exposé *Elvis: What Happened.* In that book, they divulge many of the dirty and tawdry secrets of the Elvis's life. Ed Parker told us that shortly before the book was released, Frank Sinatra had called Elvis and assured him that he (Sinatra) could stop publication of the book. Elvis thanked him but would not go along with the idea. Afterward, the King affirmed to Parker, "I don't want to be obligated to him [Sinatra]."

Expediently, insanely, Elvis and Colonel Tom Parker agreed to do a television special for CBS. It was known throughout Las Vegas that the Colonel was a heavy gambler and needed the money, while Elvis was always in financial straits during the last years of his life. A major problem was that Parker was taking an unconscionable 50 percent of the profits from Elvis, and was eventually reprimanded in court.

The King should have been in intensive care rather than giving concerts. Many of his friends doubted that he could make it through the pressure cooker of performing. Indeed, Elvis's precipitous decision was probably the first death knell. The shows were pathetic, but on two songs, "How Great Thou Art" and "Unchained Melody," Elvis somehow, some way, felt the breath of a deeper spirit move in his soul.

♦ ♦ ♦ ♦

How Great Thou Art *(From Elvis in Concert,* 1977)

In this live version, Elvis enunciates the words with pious reverence, while the high notes are stained-glass windows of emotion, the sun pouring through as if he wishes to communicate with the heavens, building to the line where he ad-libs, "*How great I think you are*, how great thou art." He changes the lyrics to emphasize that this is something he holds sacred; it is not just what someone else wrote. The Stamps stand out on this song, easily delivering their best performance as Elvis's backup singers. Their forté is clearly gospel—and nothing else.

As a student of the Bible, Elvis knew the importance of public acknowledgment, and before a television audience of 55 million, he chose to make his public commitment to God. Phil Gelormine of *Billboard* wrote, " 'How Great Thou Art' was a plea for salvation." The final "how great, how great, how great," belongs in hallowed ground.

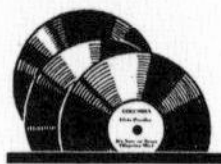

Unchained Melody *(Elvis—The Greatest Performances, Vol. I* video)

Elvis Presley sang live renditions of "Unchained Melody," but this version eclipses all the others. It is also featured on the *Elvis—The Greatest Performances* television special, which is superbly hosted and narrated by Priscilla Presley. It was recorded in June 1977, two months before his death.

Some critics didn't know what to make of this performance because it contradicts their position that Elvis was finished as an artist, so they called it melodramatic. Many critics, however, raved about it.

In describing Elvis's performances of this kind, rock critic Greil Marcus says that "for an instant, he captures the bigness, the intensity, and the unpredictability of America itself." Phil Gelormine, editor of the original *Elvis World*, wrote, "this was not mere singing, but a man's soul crying out for release from his worldly body."

This performance was filmed as part of a special for CBS, and it turned out to be Elvis's last tour. In the two shows filmed by CBS, in Omaha and Rapid City, Elvis Presley was a man to be pitied. His usual self-confidence on stage was replaced by insecurity and nervousness. He gave looks of apology throughout the concert, and moved like a man with crippling arthritis—or one so dazed and confused that he appeared to be in slow motion—his smile sad and pleading.

Besides "Unchained Melody," the two shows contained only two noteworthy numbers, "How Great Thou Art" and "Hurt." Both songs featured outstanding efforts by Elvis, but they were not necessarily exceptional.

In the history of entertainment, many actors and singers have reached deep within themselves to give stirring performances. In addition to Elvis's "If I Can Dream," examples include Marlon Brando in *On the Waterfront* and *Last Tango in Paris*, Robert DeNiro in *The Deer Hunter*, Vivian Leigh in *A Streetcar Named Desire*, Meryl Streep in *Sophie's Choice*, and Bruce Springsteen's lashing out on "Backstreets." Elvis's unleashing of "Unchained Melody" on this occasion, however, may have risen beyond them all.

As he sits at the piano, at the very beginning, Elvis signals that this is going to be something special. He seems to come alive—as if the Holy Spirit has touched his shoulder. As he begins playing the instrument, he leads the music.

The King takes full advantage of every bit of extra space that this new benediction gives him. As he sings this song, we see the real Elvis—at his best. His vocal power and resonance, his ability to reach so deeply into himself and communicate to us has never been more evident. Suddenly, in the last 35 seconds, Elvis's evocation of need reaches the edge of endurance, and he seems about to explode like a lost sun. He growls in triumph at the end, his gestures and expressions somehow filled with light, color, freedom, and confidence. At least for the moment. The ability to reach these heights of emotion is the main reason Elvis is the finest singer ever, surpassing his only competitor, the great Frank Sinatra.

It took guts for Elvis to challenge himself in this way. It was always more than talent that made Elvis the King that he was and is.

Elvis Presley is probably the most popular entertainer and icon of the 20th century. More than 750,000 people a year tour Graceland in Memphis and pay their respects at his gravesite. Annually, more people visit Elvis's final resting place (not a tourist attraction) than view John F. Kennedy's grave at Arlington National Cemetery in Washington (a major tourist venue). In 1998, more people commemorated the death of the King 21 years after his passing than marked the first anniversary of the tragic death of Princess Diana.

On the anniversary of his death, anywhere from 10,000 to 70,000 people make the pilgrimage to Memphis to pay homage to Elvis. In comparison to other cultural icons of the era, some 800 people gather in New York each year to commemorate John Lennon's death, while fewer congregate at Marilyn Monroe's memorial, and almost no one visits John Wayne's resting place.

When the United States Postal Service issued an Elvis stamp in the mid-'90s, it was the agency's most popular release ever, accounting for $124 million in sales. The only reason the postal service didn't sell many more millions was because it decided that it would be gouging the public to issue any more Presley stamps. By contrast, a recent Marilyn Monroe stamp generated sales of $46.6 million.

There are more than 500 Elvis Presley fan clubs worldwide, with a combined membership in excess of one million. There are hundreds of Elvis imitators making money portraying the King in concert. More than 700 books have been written about Elvis, and publishers would not continue to release new titles if they didn't sell. Whether it be television specials or made-for-TV movies, Elvis has set records. His videos, particularly *Elvis—The Greatest Performances, Vols. 1 and 2*, are among the industry's biggest money-makers and at one time were ranked among the Top 10 bestsellers. Memorabilia, photos, and conventions provide further proof of the King's enduring legacy.

Graceland attracts more visitors today than it did 13 years ago. The average age of visitors to Graceland is 43, and there is a strong influx of young people. Over the past several years, most young people have not been "into" Elvis, but as they enter their 30s, many of them discover the King for the first time—and are amazed that they didn't appreciate his talents sooner.

In most surveys that seek to determine the favorite entertainer of all time, or the greatest entertainer or singer of all time, Elvis usually wins in a walk. And no one spends more money on merchandise and recordings by their favorite artist than do the King's fans.

In spite of that, Elvis suffers from a serious image problem. Too many people think that the real Elvis is a fat clown who wears gaudy jumpsuits or a simple-minded beach boy of the '60s films. A large number of people see Elvis as the perverse joke that the media often portrays him to be, and far too many believe that he was only an evil-tempered, obese drug addict.

The first and best thing that can be done for Elvis Presley is to lessen the emphasis that has been placed on his later years and focus on the talent and genius that define the King. But that also means excluding other, less noble, things. Fans who read books by Elvis's alleged friends, such as Joe Esposito, Marty Lacker, Billy Smith, Lemar Fike, and many others, receive a distorted view of his life. The commercial success of such ventures—many of which rely on sensationalism and scandal to generate publicity and sales—encourages more of the same trash to be printed.

We have talked with several of these people over the past 20 years, and refer to them frequently in this book. We have tried our best to include their perspectives on the King along with our own views—not to exploit but, hopefully, to enlighten. Sadly, most of his friends never understood what Elvis was really like, the main exception being the highly intelligent and sensitive Jerry Schilling, who has not yet written a book. Perhaps he should, because he understands the depth, personality, and character of Elvis Aron Presley.

Elvis Presley's philosophy of life came down to three thoughts. He believed that in order to be happy, a person must have something to do, someone to love, and something to look forward to. He told his wife Priscilla, "If you don't create the event, you'll never have the moment." Finally, he commented that, "Positive thinking is essential to a successful life."

Among the few books currently on the market that paint a realistic portrait of the King are Peter Guralnick's *Last Train to Memphis* and Todd Rheingold's *Dispelling the Myths*. Also, Greil Marcus's stunning *Mystery Train* is the best rock 'n' roll criticism ever written. Just as brilliant was a lecture Marcus gave on Elvis in 1981 in Memphis, which he reprinted in a book, *The Dead Elvis*. However, he left so much out (many sentences were cut in half), assuming that people would understand, that the lecture presented there is a waste of time. Try to get a tape of the original lecture on the bootleg market; it is revelatory.

RCA has done a much better job of presenting the King's career, with Ernst Jorgensen involved in coordinating music packages, but the record company has in its vaults one of the greatest rock 'n' roll albums ever made: the original recordings of the sit-down shows from the Burbank sessions. However, for whatever reason, RCA has not released the album.

Elvis Presley is deserving of the same kind of respect that is showered on the Beatles and Frank Sinatra—but without the ridicule the King alone suffers. He was a spotlight for the modern world, a seminal and revolutionary American artist. We should not allow his final, desperate years to unduly taint those achievements; rather, we should view those years as something that made Elvis all the more human, proof that he was one of us.

The huge crowds in Memphis for the 20th anniversary of Elvis's death—particularly at the candlelight vigil—were larger than those that descended on the city for the 10th anniversary of his passing. It is our hope that they represent the beginning of a new era in which the true genius and talent of Elvis Presley will not only be recognized but also celebrated.

James Treires has come closest to capturing the reason behind the fanaticism that surrounds the legend of the King. Treires wrote in a column in the early '80s:

> Elvis Presley communicates the power, the passion and the pain of living in a way that no other popular vocalist approaches. . . . Elvis Presley was perhaps too deeply aware of life to have endured too much of it. This dark, brooding quality is in his music, and those who do not respond to it have not truly lived. In Elvis's fantastic voice, that moved effortlessly from the tender touching highs to the primitive, powerful lower depths of the soul, there is contained all the turmoil, torment, and passion that makes life the glory that it is.

That is why Elvis Presley will always be the King.

But even with his genius, Elvis would not have been one of the true phenomena of the century if he were not also a remarkable, complex person. Of course, without his talent, it would all have been for naught. The combination of these elements is the reason for the fanatical following the King has always enjoyed.

We believe that the analyses contained in this book will

demonstrate that Elvis Presley was a great artist not just for four years in the 1950s but throughout his career. To conclude *The Essential Elvis* on the down note the media relentlessly enforces would be a mistake; indeed, to accept the idea that the life and career of Elvis Presley were a failure would be a tragic injustice. As noted music critic Dave Marsh stated on a Casey Kasem television special about the King, "Elvis's story is the greatest success story I've ever seen." There is considerably more to Elvis Presley's life and career than just his last few years.

Elvis the person was a flawed but good man. His generosity and kindness were rare in a business where those qualities are seldom found. It is a credit to the King that at no point in his career did he forget where he came from. Many in show business claim that they have never lost the essence of who they once were, but this is true of only a very few. Many entertainers have become so popular that they have come to believe they are above the masses and, in countless cases, have become conglomerates. It is a tribute to the King that one cannot think of Elvis and the word "conglomerate" together without laughing at the absurdity. One of the reasons for his demise was because he cared and felt too much.

Even at the end, wallowing in self-destruction, Elvis Presley remained a humanitarian. For example, shortly before his death, he called former Pennsylvania Governor Milton Shapp to ask how he could help aid the victims of a terrible flood in that state. Only after his death did the number of charities he had endowed become public knowledge. The list is extensive.

Elvis was good to people; he loved "family," and loyalty meant a great deal to him. Yes, he made mistakes, but all human beings do. Even when he was sick and dying, Elvis always treated his fans well—and with respect.

It got to the point that being Elvis Presley was one of the hardest jobs in the world. None of us can relate to that because it is doubtful than any other individual has ever experienced so much popularity and adulation.

In the end, nothing can take away from the fact that Elvis Presley was a working-class hero because he dared to be different. Even though he was often criticized for his independence and rebelliousness, Elvis continued to express his uniqueness and open the doors to social freedom.

The King was the fiercest hurricane in music and popular culture in the 20th century. He still touches our hearts and souls in profound and gentle ways that revive our spirits and rekindle our faith in the future.

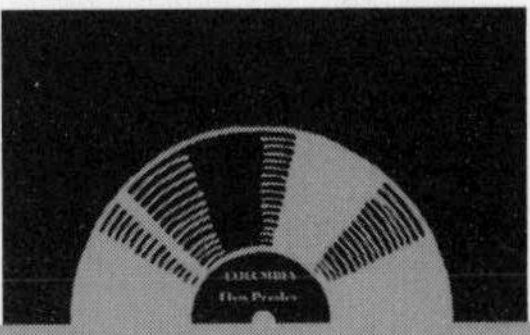

DISCOGRAPHY

Many fine Elvis Presley boxed sets have been released by RCA, but nothing is available for prospective fans that demonstrates the range and depth of the King's talent.

There are so many uneven albums on the market, and a glut of poorly made films, that many potential Elvis aficionados are often turned off before they have a chance to experience what he really has to offer, as we have discovered through our surveys. RCA and the Elvis Presley estate need to put out a boxed set of recordings that will demonstrate the diversity of Elvis's talent. It should be a truly definitive anthology that will appeal to everyone, especially younger music lovers. Such a boxed set must be selective, but it should also be the first of many new releases. For instance, a few cuts should be offered from *Elvis Is Back* and *From Elvis in Memphis*. Once listeners hear these songs, they will probably have to have both albums.

The following 50 songs best illustrate the variety of Elvis's career for new and seasoned listeners. This is not a "greatest hits" list. (Note: All of the following selections are available on RCA, except for "Unchained Melody.")

1. That's All Right (Mama)
2. Good Rockin' Tonight
3. Mystery Train
4. Heartbreak Hotel

5. Hound Dog
6. Don't Be Cruel
7. Love Me Tender
8. All Shook Up
9. Rip It Up
10. Ready Teddy
11. Teddy Bear
12. Blue Suede Shoes
13. When My Blue Moon Turns to Gold Again
14. Long Tall Sally
15. Jailhouse Rock
16. (You're So Square) Baby I Don't Care
17. I Need Your Love Tonight
18. Fame and Fortune
19. Fever
20. Reconsider Baby
21. Now or Never
22. Can't Help Falling in Love
23. (Marie's the Name) His Latest Flame
24. Little Sister
25. Hi-Heel Sneakers
26. Lawdy, Miss Clawdy (from *Elvis* [NBC] and *Elvis* [RCA])
27. If I Can Dream
28. Wearin' That Loved On Look
29. In the Ghetto
30. Suspicious Minds
31. Kentucky Rain
32. The Wonder of You
33. This Is Our Dance
34. Early Morning Rain
35. Promised Land
36. I've Lost You (long version from *Elvis: The Other Sides*)
37. Tomorrow Is a Long Time
38. You've Lost That Lovin' Feeling
39. Honky Tonk Angel
40. Snowbird
41. Always On My Mind

42. She Thinks I Still Care
43. Pieces of My Life
44. Hurt
45. Little Darlin'
46. Merry Christmas Baby (from the 1971 Christmas album)
47. Moody Blue
48. You'll Never Walk Alone
49. How Great Thou Art (studio version)
50. Unchained Melody (from *Elvis—The Greatest Performances, Vol. 1* video, 1990)

Songs Analyzed in *The Essential Elvis*

The following listing of all the songs analyzed in The Essential Elvis *includes the album or CD on which each appears, the year it was released, and the songwriter(s). In some cases, a particular song may appear on several CDs or cassettes, but in most cases we have chosen to list only the album or albums on which it is best heard. The page number at the end of each listing indicates where the song analysis can be found.*

That's All Right (Mama) (*The Complete Sun Sessions,* 1987, and *King of Rock 'N' Roll* boxed set, 1992), Crudup, page 4

Good Rockin' Tonight (*The Complete Sun Sessions,* 1987, and *King of Rock 'N' Roll* boxed set, 1992), Brown, page 6

Blue Moon of Kentucky (*The Complete Sun Sessions,* 1987, and *King of Rock 'N' Roll* boxed set, 1992), Monroe, page 7

Baby, Let's Play House (*The Complete Sun Sessions,* 1987, and *King of Rock 'N' Roll* boxed set, 1992), Brown, page 8

Milkcow Blues Boogie (*The Complete Sun Sessions,* 1987, and *King of Rock 'N' Roll* boxed set, 1992), Arnold, page 10

I'm Left, You're Right, She's Gone (*The Complete Sun Sessions,* 1987, and *King of Rock 'N' Roll* boxed set, 1992), Kesler-Taylor, page 11

Mystery Train (*The Complete Sun Sessions,* 1987, and *King of Rock 'N' Roll* boxed set, 1992), Parker-Phillips, page 14

Trying to Get to You (*The Complete Sun Sessions,* 1987, and *King of Rock 'N' Roll* boxed set, 1992), Singleton-McCoy, page 15

Blue Moon (*The Complete Sun Sessions,* 1987, and *King of Rock 'N' Roll* boxed set, 1992), Rodgers-Hart, page 15

Heartbreak Hotel (*Elvis's Golden Records, Vol. 1,* 1997, and *King of Rock 'N' Roll* boxed set, 1992), Axton-Durden-Presley, page 25 (**Note:** Elvis had nothing to do with writing this song, although he produced the sound.)

I Was the One (*Elvis's Golden Records, Vol. 1,* 1997, and *King of Rock 'N' Roll* boxed set, 1992), Schroeder-DeMatruis-Blair-Petters, page 26

Hound Dog (*Elvis's Golden Records, Vol. 1,* 1997, and *King of Rock 'N' Roll* boxed set, 1992), J. Leiber-M. Stoller, page 27 (**Note:** Elvis should have been given writer's credit for the version of "Hound Dog" he released, which is nothing like the song Leiber and Stoller wrote.)

Don't Be Cruel (*Elvis's Golden Records, Vol. 1,* 1997, and *King of Rock 'N' Roll* boxed set, 1992), Otis Blackwell-Elvis Presley, page 32

Tutti Frutti (*Elvis '56,* 1996 and *King of Rock 'N' Roll* boxed set, 1992), Dorothy Labostrie-Richard Penniman, page 35

Money Honey (*King of Rock 'N' Roll* boxed set, 1992), Jesse Stone, page 36

Too Much (*Elvis's Golden Records, Vol. 1,* and *King of Rock 'N' Roll* boxed set, 1992), Lee Rosenberg-Bernard Weinman, page 37

All Shook Up (*Elvis's Golden Records, Vol. 1,* and *King of Rock 'N' Roll* boxed set, 1992), Otis Blackwell-Elvis Presley, page 38

Love Me Tender (*Elvis's Golden Records, Vol. 1,* 1997, and *King of Rock 'N' Roll* boxed set, 1992), Vera Matson-Elvis Presley, page 41

Good Luck Charm (*Elvis's Golden Records, Vol. 3,* 1997, and *From Nashville to Memphis* boxed set, 1993), Aaron Schroeder-Wallie Gold, page 42

Teddy Bear (*Elvis's Golden Records, Vol. 1,* 1997, and *King of Rock 'N' Roll* boxed set, 1992), Kal Mann-Bernie Lowe, page 42

When My Blue Moon Turns to Gold Again (*King of Rock 'N' Roll* boxed set, 1992), W. Walker-G. Sullivan, page 43

Ready Teddy (*Elvis '56,* 1996, and *King of Rock 'N' Roll* boxed set, 1992), R. Blackwell-J. Marascaleo, page 44

Blue Suede Shoes (*King of Rock 'N' Roll* boxed set, 1992), Carl Perkins, page 44

Rip It Up (*Elvis '56,* 1996, and *King of Rock 'N' Roll* boxed set, 1992), R. Blackwell-J. Marascaleo, page 47

Long Tall Sally (*King of Rock 'N' Roll* boxed set, 1992), R. Blackwell-J. Marascaleo, page 48

Jailhouse Rock (*Elvis's Golden Records, Vol. 1,* 1997, and *King of Rock 'N' Roll* boxed set, 1992), Jerry Leiber-Mike Stoller, page 49

(You're So Square) Baby I Don't Care (*Jailhouse Rock/Love Me Tender,* 1997, and *King of Rock 'N' Roll* boxed set, 1992), Jerry Leiber-Mike Stoller, page 50

I Beg of You (*Essential Elvis, Vol. 2,* 1988, and *King of Rock 'N' Roll* boxed set, 1992), Rosemarie McCoy-Kelly Owens, page 50

Trouble (*King Creole,* 1997, and *King of Rock 'N' Roll* boxed set, 1992), Jerry Leiber-Mike Stoller, page 52

One Night of Sin (*King of Rock 'N' Roll* boxed set, 1992), D. Bartholomew-P. King, page 53

I Need Your Love Tonight (*Elvis's Golden Records, Vol. 2,* 1997, and *King of Rock 'N' Roll* boxed set, 1992), Wayne Reichner, page 54

Fame and Fortune (*Elvis's Golden Records, Vol. 3,* and *From Nashville to Memphis,* 1993, Wise-Weisman, page 58

Make Me Know It (*Elvis Is Back,* 1960, and *From Nashville to Memphis,* 1993), Otis Blackwell, page 60

Fever (*Elvis Is Back,* 1960, and *From Nashville to Memphis,* 1993), Davenport-Cooley, page 61

Such a Night (*Elvis Is Back,* 1960, and *From Nashville to Memphis,* 1993), Chase, page 62

Like a Baby (*Elvis Is Back,* 1960, and *From Nashville to Memphis,* 1993), Stone, page 63

Reconsider Baby (*Elvis Is Back,* 1960, and *From Nashville to Memphis,* 1993), Lowell Fulson, page 63

Now or Never (*Elvis's Golden Records, Vol. 3,* 1997), Aaron Schroeder-Wally Gold, page 66

Are You Lonesome Tonight? (*Elvis's Golden Records, Vol. 3,* 1997), Roy Turk-Lou Handman, page 67

Can't Help Falling in Love (*Elvis: Worldwide 50 Gold Award Hits, Vol. 1,* 1970, and *Blue Hawaii,* 1997), Peretti-Creatore-Weiss, page 68

Rock-A-Hula Baby (*Blue Hawaii,* 1997), Wise-Weisman-Fuller, page 69

(Marie's the Name) His Latest Flame (*Elvis's Golden Records, Vol. 3,* 1997, and *From Nashville to Memphis,* 1993), Doc Pomus-Mort Shuman, page 72

Little Sister (*Elvis's Golden Records, Vol. 3,* 1997, and *From Nashville to Memphis,* 1993), Doc Pomus-Mort Shuman, page 72

Surrender (*Elvis's Golden Records, Vol. 3,* 1997, and *From Nashville to Memphis,* 1993), Doc Pomus-Mort Shuman, page 75

Return to Sender (*Elvis's Golden Records, Vol. 3,* 1997), Otis Blackwell, page 76

It Hurts Me (*Elvis's Golden Records, Vol. 4,* 1997, and *From Nashville to Memphis,* 1993), Byers, page 76

Devil in Disguise (*Elvis's Golden Records, Vol. 4,* 1997, and *From Nashville to Memphis,* 1993), Giant-Baum-Kaye, page 78

Memphis (*Elvis for Everyone,* 1965, and *From Nashville to Memphis,* 1993), Chuck Berry, page 81

For the Millionth and Last Time (*Elvis for Everyone,* 1965, and *From Nashville to Memphis,* 1993), Roy Bennett-Sid Tepper, page 82

It Keeps Right On A Hurtin' (*From Elvis in Memphis,* 1969), Johnny Tillitson, page 122

After Lovin' You (*From Elvis in Memphis,* 1969), E. Miller-J. Lantz, page 123

In the Ghetto (*From Elvis in Memphis,* 1969), Scott-David, page 123

Rubberneckin' (*Collector's Gold,* 1991), Dory Jones-Bunny Warren, page 125

Kentucky Rain (*Elvis's Golden Records, Vol. 5,* 1997, and *From Nashville to Memphis,* 1993), Eddie Rabbitt-D. Heard, page 126

Suspicious Minds (*Elvis's Golden Records, Vol. 5,* 1997, and *Elvis's Greatest Hits,* 1981), Mark James, page 127

The Wonder of You (*February 1970 On Stage,* 1970, and *Walk a Mile in My Shoes* '70s boxed set, 1995), Knight, page 137

Polk Salad Annie (**Note:** The reviewed version is not on any album, but a great rendition can be heard on *February 1970 On Stage,* 1970), Tony Joe White, page 137

I've Lost You (*Elvis: The Other Sides; Worldwide Gold Award Hits, Vol. 2,* 1971, and *Walk a Mile in My Shoes* '70s boxed set, 1995), Howard-Blakley, page 137

Bridge Over Troubled Water (*Walk a Mile in My Shoes* '70s boxed set, 1995), Paul Simon, page 141

You've Lost that Lovin' Feelin' (*Elvis: That's the Way It Is,* 1970), Barry Mann-Cynthia Well, page 142

Mary in the Morning (*Elvis: That's the Way It Is,* 1970), Johnny Cymbal-Michael Rashkow, page 146

Walk a Mile in My Shoes (*February 1970 On Stage,* 1970, and *Walk a Mile in My Shoes* '70s boxed set, 1995), Joe South, page 147

Snowbird (*Elvis Country,* 1971, and *Walk a Mile in My Shoes* '70s boxed set, 1995), Gene MacLellen, page 148

Whole Lotta Shakin' (*Elvis Country,* 1971, and *Walk a Mile in My Shoes* '70s boxed set, 1995), Dave Williams-Sonny David, page 148

This Is Our Dance (*Love Letters,* 1971), Les Reed-Geoff Stephens, page 149

I Really Don't Want to Know (*Elvis Country,* 1971, and *Walk a Mile in My Shoes* '70s boxed set, 1995), Barnes-Robertson, page 150

Help Me Make It Through the Night (*Elvis Now,* 1972), Kris Kristofferson, page 151

Hey Jude (*Elvis Now,* 1972), John Lennon-Paul McCartney, page 152

Merry Christmas Baby (*Elvis Sings the Wonderful World of Christmas,* 1971), L. Baxter-J. Moore, page 153

Burning Love (*Elvis's Greatest Hits,* 1981; *Elvis's Golden Records, Vol. 5,* 1997; and *Walk a Mile in My Shoes* '70s boxed set, 1995), Dennis Linde, page 155

I'm So Lonesome I Could Cry (*Aloha from Hawaii,* 1973), Hank Williams, page 159

American Trilogy (*Aloha from Hawaii,* 1973), Mickey Newberry, page 160

Find Out What's Happening (*Raised on Rock,* 1973), Crutchfield, page 163

Promised Land (*Promised Land,* 1975, and *Walk a Mile in My Shoes* '70s boxed set, 1995), Chuck Berry, page 165

It's Midnight (*Promised Land,* 1975, and *Walk a Mile in My Shoes* '70s boxed set, 1995), Billy Edd Wheeler-Jerry Chestnut, page 168

Honky Tonk Angel (*Promised Land,* 1975), Troy Seals-Denny Rice, page 169

T-R-O-U-B-L-E (*Elvis Today,* 1975, and *Walk a Mile in My Shoes* '70s boxed set, 1995), Jerry Chestnut, page 172

My Way (*Walk a Mile in My Shoes* '70s boxed set, 1995), Paul Anka, page 173

Always On My Mind (*Walk a Mile in My Shoes* '70s boxed set, 1995), Thompson-James-Christopher, page 175

Pieces of My Life (*Elvis Today,* 1975, and *Walk a Mile in My Shoes* '70s boxed set, 1995), Troy Seals, page 176

Hurt (*From Elvis Presley Boulevard, Memphis, Tennessee,* 1976), Crane-Jacobs, page 177

For the Heart (*From Elvis Presley Boulevard, Memphis, Tennessee,* 1976), Dennis Linde, page 178

Moody Blue (*Moody Blue,* 1977, and *Walk a Mile in My Shoes* '70s boxed set, 1995), Mark James, page 178

Little Darlin' (*Moody Blue,* 1977), Williams, page 181

Way Down (*Moody Blue,* 1977, and *Walk a Mile in My Shoes* '70s boxed set, 1995), Martine Jr., page 181

She Thinks I Still Care (*Moody Blue,* 1977, and *Walk a Mile in My Shoes* '70s boxed set, 1995), Lee, page 182

How Great Thou Art (live version from *Elvis in Concert,* 1977), Hine, page 184

Unchained Melody (*Elvis—The Greatest Performances, Vol. 1* video, 1990), North-Zaret, page 184

SINGLES

The singles released during Elvis Presley's lifetime are listed below in chronological order, "A" side first. Numbers in parentheses refer to the highest position reached on Billboard's *Honor Roll of Hits, Top 100, and Hot 100 singles charts. The Hot 100 debuted in the publication's August 4, 1958, issue.*

That's All Right (Mama) / Blue Moon of Kentucky, August 1954

Good Rockin' Tonight / I Don't Care if the Sun Don't Shine, October 1954

Mikcow Blues Boogie / You're a Heartbreaker, January 1955

I'm Left, You're Right, She's Gone / Baby, Let's Play House, May 1955

Mystery Train / I Forgot to Remember to Forget, August 1955

Heartbreak Hotel / I Was the One, January 1956 (1)

I Want You, I Need You, I Love You / My Baby Left Me, May 1956 (3)

Hound Dog / Don't Be Cruel, July 1956 (1) / (1)

Blue Suede Shoes / Tutti Frutti, September 1956 (24)

I'm Counting on You / I Got a Woman, September 1956

I'll Never Let You Go / I'm Gonna Sit Right Down and Cry Over You, September 1956

Tryin' to Get to You / I Love You Because, September 1956

Blue Moon / Just Because, September 1956 (55)

Money Honey / One-Sided Love Affair, September 1956 (76)

Shake, Rattle and Roll / Lawdy, Miss Clawdy, September 1956

Love Me Tender / Any Way You Want Me, September 1956 (1)

Too Much / Playing for Keeps, January 1957 (1)

All Shook Up / That's When Your Heartaches Begin, March 1957 (1)

Teddy Bear / Loving You, June 1957 (1)

Jailhouse Rock / Treat Me Nice, September 1957 (1)

Don't / I Beg of You, December 1957 (1)

Wear My Ring Around Your Neck / Doncha' Think It's Time, April 1958 (3)

Hard-Headed Woman / Don't Ask Me Why, June 1958 (2)

I Got Stung / One Night, October 1958 (8)

A Fool Such As I / I Need Your Love Tonight, March 1959 (2)

A Big Hunk O' Love / My Wish Came True, June 1959 (1)

Stuck On You / Fame and Fortune, March 1960 (1)

It's Now or Never / A Mess of Blues, July 1960 (1)

Are You Lonesome Tonight? / I Gotta Know, November 1960 (1)

Surrender / Lonely Man, February 1961 (1)

I Feel So Bad / Wild in the Country, May 1961 (5)

Little Sister / His Latest Flame, August 1961 (5)

Can't Help Falling in Love / Rock-a-Hula Baby, November 1961 (2)

Good Luck Charm / Anything That's Part of You, February 1962 (1)

She's Not You / Just Tell Her Jim Said Hello, July 1962 (5)

Return to Sender / Where Do You Come From?, October 1962 (2)

One Broken Heart for Sale / They Remind Me Too Much of You, January 1963 (11)

(You're the) Devil in Disguise / Please Don't Drag That String Around, June 1963 (3)

Bossa Nova Baby / Witchcraft, October 1963 (8)

Kissin' Cousins / It Hurts Me, October 1963 (12)

Kiss Me Quick / Suspicion, April 1964 (34)

Viva Las Vegas / What'd I Say, April 1964 (29)

Such a Night / Never Ending, July 1964 (16)

Ain't That Loving You, Baby / Ask Me, September 1964 (16)

Blue Christmas / Wooden Heart, November 1964

Do the Clam / You'll Be Gone, March 1965 (21)

Crying in the Chapel / I Believe in the Man in the Sky, April 1965 (3)

(Such an) Easy Question / If Feels So Right, May 1965 (11)

Puppet on a String / Wooden Heart, August 1965 (14)

Blue Christmas / Santa Claus Is Back in Town, November 1965

Tell Me Why / Blue River, January 1966 (33)

Joshua Fit the Battle / Known Only to Him, February 1966

Milky White Way / Swing Down Sweet Chariot, February 1966

Frankie and Johnny / Please Don't Stop Loving Me, March 1966 (25)

Love Letters / Come What May, June 1966 (19)

Spinout / All That I Am, October 1966 (40)

If Every Day Was Like Christmas / How Would You Like to Be, November 1966

Indescribably Blue / Fools Fall in Love, January 1967 (33)

Long Legged Girl / That's Someone You Never Forget, May 1967 (63)

There's Always Me / Judy, August 1967 (56)

Big Boss Man / You Don't Know Me, September 1967 (38)

Guitar Man / Hi-Heel Sneakers, January 1968 (43)

U.S. Male / Stay Away, Joe, March 1968 (28)

You'll Never Walk Alone / We Call on Him, April 1968 (90)

Let Yourself Go / Your Time Hasn't Come Yet, Baby, May 1968 (71)

A Little Less Conversation / Almost in Love, September 1968 (63)

If I Can Dream / Edge of Reality, October 1968 (12)

Memories / Charro, March 1969 (35)

How Great Thou Art / His Hand in Mine, April 1969

In the Ghetto / Any Day Now, April 1969 (3)

Clean Up Your Own Back Yard / The Fair Is Moving On, June 1969 (35)

Suspicious Minds / You'll Think of Me, August 1969 (1)

Don't Cry Daddy / Rubberneckin', November 1969 (6)

Kentucky Rain / My Little Friend, January 1970 (16)

The Wonder of You / Mama Liked the Roses, May 1970 (9)

I've Lost You / The Next Step Is Love, July 1970 (32)

You Don't Have to Say You Love Me / Patch It Up, October 1970 (11)

I Really Don't Want to Know / There Goes My Everything, December 1970 (21)

Rags to Riches / Where Did They Go, Lord, March 1971 (33)

Life / Only Believe, May 1971 (53)

I'm Leavin' / Heart of Rome, August 1971 (36)

It's Only Love / The Sound of Your Cry, October 1971 (51)

Merry Christmas, Baby / O Come, All Ye Faithful, November 1971

Until It's Time for You to Go / We Can Make the Morning, January 1972 (40)

He Touched Me / The Bosom of Abraham, March 1972

An American Trilogy / The First Time I Saw Your Face, May 1972 (66)

Burning Love / It's a Matter of Time, August 1972 (2)

Always On My Mind / Separate Ways, November 1972 (20)

Fool / Steamroller Blues, March 1973 (17)

Raised on Rock / For ol' Times Sake, September 1973 (41)

Take Good Care of Her / I've Got a Thing About You, Baby, January 1974 (39)

Help Me / You Talk in Your Sleep, May 1974 (17)

Promised Land / It's Midnight, October 1974 (14)

My Boy / Thinking About You, January 1975 (20)

T-R-O-U-B-L-E / Mr. Songman, April 1975 (35)

Bringing It Back / Pieces of My Life, October 1975 (65)

Hurt / For the Heart, March 1976 (20)

Moody Blue / She Thinks I Still Care, December 1976 (31)

Way Down / Pledging My Love, June 1977 (21)

ALBUMS

The albums released during Elvis Presley's lifetime are listed below by date of release. Also included is the highest chart position reached on Billboard's *album chart.*

Elvis Presley, April 1956 (1)

Elvis, October 1956 (1)

Loving You, July 1957 (1)

Elvis's Christmas Album, November 1957 (1)

Elvis's Golden Records, March 1958 (3)

King Creole, August 1958 (2)

For LP Fans Only, February 1959 (23)

A Date with Elvis, August 1959 (32)

50,000,000 Elvis Fans Can't Be Wrong: Elvis's Gold Records Vol. 2, (31)

Elvis Is Back, April 1959 (2)

G.I. Blues, October 1960 (1)

His Hand in Mine, December 1960 (87)

Something for Everybody, June 1961 (1)

Blue Hawaii, October 1961 (1)

Pot Luck, June 1962 (4)

Girls! Girls! Girls!, November 1962 (3)

It Happened at the World's Fair, March 1963 (4)

Elvis' Golden Records, Vol. 3, September 1963 (4)

Fun in Acapulco, November 1963 (3)

Kissin' Cousins, March 1964 (6)

Roustabout, October 1964 (1)

Girl Happy, April 1965 (8)

Elvis for Everyone, July 1965 (10)

Harum Scarum, October 1965 (8)

Frankie and Johnny, April 1966 (20)

Paradise, Hawaiian Style, June 1966 (15)

Spinout, October 1966 (18)

How Great Thou Art, March 1967 (18)

Double Trouble, June 1967 (47)

Clambake, November 1967 (40)

Elvis's Gold Records, Vol. 4, February 1968 (33)

Speedway, June 1968 (82)

Elvis Singing "Flaming Star" and Others, November 1968

Elvis (NBC-TV special), December 1968 (8)

From Elvis in Memphis, May 1969 (13)

From Memphis to Vegas / From Vegas to Memphis (two-record set), November 1969 (12)

February 1970 On Stage, May 1970 (13)

Elvis: Worldwide 50 Gold Award Hits, Vol. 1, August 1970 (45)

Back in Memphis, November 1970 (183)

Elvis: That's the Way It Is, December 1970 (21)

Elvis Country, January 1971 (12)

Love Letters from Elvis, June 1971 (33)

Elvis: The Other Sides; Worldwide Gold Award Hits, Vol. 2, August 1971 (120)

The Wonderful World of Christmas, October 1971

Elvis Now, January 1972 (43)

He Touched Me, April 1972

Elvis as Recorded at Madison Square Garden, June 1972 (11)

Elvis: Aloha from Hawaii, February 1973 (1)

Elvis, June 1973 (52)

Raised on Rock, October 1973 (50)

A Legendary Performer, Vol. 1, January 1974 (43)

Good Times, March 1974 (90)

Elvis: Recorded Live on Stage in Memphis, June 1974 (33)

Having Fun with Elvis on Stage, October 1974 (130)

Promised Land, Janurary 1975 (47)

Pure Gold, March 1975

Elvis Today, June 1975 (57)

A Legendary Performer, Vol. 2, January 1976 (50)

His Hand in Mine, March 1967

The Sun Sessions, March 1976 (48)

From Elvis Presley Boulevard, Memphis, Tennessee, May 1976 (41)

Welcome to My World, March 1977 (44)

Moody Blue, June 1977 (3)

Samuel Roy has written columns on rock music for *America Today* and *Rock N' Roll Today*. The author of two books, *Elvis: Prophet of Power* and *Visions*, he is a graduate of Duquesne University and plays several musical instruments, including guitar.

Tom Aspell has been an instructor of college composition and literature for 18 years and currently teaches at the University of Pittsburgh and the Community College of Allegheny County, Pennsylvania, focusing on popular culture. He has written a column on rock music for *America Today*.